barbecue

HOMESTYLE

barbecue

MURDOCH BOOKS

contents

Barbecue bliss

Invite friends and family over for a barbecue and it's unlikely they'll refuse. After all, who can possibly resist those rich, smoky aromas and the crunchy, crusty, juicy deliciousness of food cooked over the coals (or gas or wood)? A barbecue puts everyone in a good mood—even the cook, as barbecuing has to be one of the most fuss-free methods of cooking known to man. All you need is a half-decent barbecue and a few pieces of simple equipment (tongs, bowls and the like) and you're ready; in fact, you don't even require a backyard as it's quite possible to barbecue on a spacious balcony.

The hardest part of hosting a barbecue is deciding what to throw on it. Burgers, kebabs, steak or sausages are all obvious choices, but they're just the beginning … will it be chicken tikka kebabs, spicy burgers or rump steak? Then there are the myriad fish, pork and vegetarian options to consider; after all, sardines, prawns, snapper and calamari cook happily on the barbecue, as do vegetable-laden skewers and the many tender cuts of pork. Endless sauce and accompaniment possibilities make for even more choices to ponder, such as peanut sauce for satay, capsicum salsa

for cheeseburgers, pistachio couscous for Moroccan lamb, as well as innumerable side-dish options (chargrilled asparagus, tabouleh, stir-fried salad or warm marinated mushroom salad, for example). In fact, when planning a 'barbie', it soon becomes clear that there's more to think about than just the meat.

Of course the meat is the main event (no argument there!), but it stands or falls on what you put with it, and the recipes in this book, whether for a crisp, leafy salad or a bubbling potato and tomato gratin, have been specially selected because they're simple to prepare while the barbecue is firing up. As have the desserts, because the sweet course shouldn't be overlooked either. When you're barbecuing, the best dessert is one that you can whip up beforehand. Pass the disposable plates, laden with something simple, cool and fruity (ginger and lychee jelly or mandarin ice maybe) or morsels of an altogether more decadent persuasion (mmmm, baked cheesecake or chocolate mousse flan), and they'll all go home happy. And so will you be, at clean-up time, with no dishes to do! Surely the best feature of any barbecue!

Dips

Guacamole

PREPARATION TIME: 30 MINUTES | TOTAL COOKING TIME: NIL | SERVES 6

3 ripe avocados
1 tablespoon lime or lemon juice
    (see HINT)
1 tomato
1–2 red chillies, finely chopped
1 small red onion, finely chopped
1 tablespoon finely chopped coriander
    (cilantro) leaves
2 tablespoons sour cream
1–2 drops Tabasco or habañero sauce
corn chips, to serve

1 Roughly chop the avocado flesh and place in a bowl. Mash lightly with a fork and sprinkle with the lime or lemon juice to prevent the avocado from discolouring.

2 Cut the tomato in half horizontally and use a teaspoon to scoop out the seeds. Finely dice the flesh and add to the avocado.

3 Stir in the chilli, onion, coriander, sour cream and Tabasco or habañero sauce. Season with freshly cracked black pepper.

4 Serve immediately or cover the surface with plastic wrap and refrigerate for 1–2 hours. If refrigerated, allow to come to room temperature before serving. Serve with corn chips.

HINT: You will need 1–2 limes to produce 1 tablespoon of juice, depending on the lime. A heavier lime will probably be juicier. To get more juice from a citrus fruit, prick it all over with a fork and then heat on High (100%) in the microwave for 1 minute. Don't forget to prick it or the fruit may burst.

NUTRITION PER SERVE
Protein 3 g; Fat 30 g; Carbohydrate 2 g; Dietary Fibre 3 g; Cholesterol 9 mg; 1200 kJ (290 Cal)

Use disposable gloves when chopping chilli to avoid skin irritation.

Remove the avocado stone by tapping onto it with a sharp knife and lifting up.

Cut the tomato in half horizontally and scoop out the seeds with a teaspoon.

Hummus

PREPARATION TIME: 20 MINUTES + OVERNIGHT SOAKING | TOTAL COOKING TIME: 1 HOUR 15 MINUTES | SERVES 20

220 g (7¾ oz/1 cup) dried chickpeas
2 tablespoons tahini (sesame paste)
4 garlic cloves, crushed
2 teaspoons ground cumin
4 tablespoons lemon juice
3 tablespoons olive oil
large pinch cayenne pepper
extra lemon juice, optional
extra olive oil, to garnish
paprika, to garnish
chopped flat-leaf (Italian) parsley, to garnish
pitta bread or pide (Turkish/flat bread),
    to serve

1 Soak the chickpeas in 1 litre (35 fl oz/4 cups) water overnight. Drain and place in a large saucepan with 2 litres (70 fl oz/8 cups) fresh water (enough to cover the chickpeas by 5 cm/ 2 inches). Bring to the boil, then reduce the heat and simmer for 1 hour 15 minutes, or until the chickpeas are very tender. Skim any froth from the surface. Drain well, reserve the cooking liquid and leave until cool enough to handle. Pick over for any loose skins and discard.

2 Process the chickpeas, tahini, garlic, cumin, lemon juice, olive oil, cayenne pepper and 1½ teaspoons salt in a food processor until thick and smooth. With the motor still running, gradually add about 185 ml (6 fl oz/¾ cup) reserved cooking liquid to form a smooth creamy purée. Season with salt or extra lemon juice.

3 Scoop into a bowl, drizzle with oil, sprinkle with paprika and scatter the parsley over the top. Serve with pitta bread or pide that has been warmed on the barbecue.

Pick through the cooled chickpeas to remove any loose skins.

Process the chickpea mixture with the reserved cooking liquid until creamy.

NUTRITION PER SERVE
Protein 1.2 g; Fat 4.7 g; Carbohydrate 1.6 g; Dietary Fibre 0.9 g; Cholesterol 0 mg; 228 kJ (54 Cal)

Tzatziki

PREPARATION TIME: 10 MINUTES + 15 MINUTES STANDING | TOTAL COOKING TIME: NIL | SERVES 12

2 Lebanese (short) cucumbers
400 g (14 oz) Greek-style yoghurt
4 garlic cloves, crushed
3 tablespoons finely chopped mint, plus extra
    to garnish
1 tablespoon lemon juice
pitta bread or pide (Turkish/flat bread),
    to serve

1 Cut the cucumbers in half lengthways, scoop out the seeds and discard. Leave the skin on and coarsely grate the cucumber into a small colander. Sprinkle with salt and leave over a large bowl for 15 minutes to drain off any bitter juices.

2 Meanwhile, stir together the yoghurt, crushed garlic, mint and lemon juice.

3 Rinse the cucumber under cold water then, taking small handfuls, squeeze out any excess moisture. Combine the grated cucumber with the yoghurt mixture and season well. Serve immediately with pitta bread or pide.

STORAGE: *Will keep in an airtight container in the fridge for 2–3 days.*

NUTRITION PER SERVE
Protein 1.6 g; Fat 1.2 g; Carbohydrate 2.3 g; Dietary
Fibre 0.5 g; Cholesterol 5.3 mg; 119 kJ (28 Cal)

Cut the cucumbers in half and scoop out the seeds with a teaspoon.

Mix the yoghurt, crushed garlic, mint and lemon juice together.

Squeeze the grated cucumber to remove any excess moisture.

Baba ghanoush

PREPARATION TIME: 20 MINUTES + 30 MINUTES COOLING | TOTAL COOKING TIME: 50 MINUTES | SERVES 10

2 eggplants (aubergines)
3 garlic cloves, crushed
½ teaspoon ground cumin
4 tablespoons lemon juice
2 tablespoons tahini (sesame paste)
pinch cayenne pepper
1½ tablespoons olive oil
1 tablespoon finely chopped flat-leaf
    (Italian) parsley
black olives, to garnish
pitta bread or pide (Turkish/flat bread),
    to serve

NUTRITION PER SERVE
Protein 1.8 g; Fat 5 g; Carbohydrate 3 g; Dietary
Fibre 3 g; Cholesterol 0 mg; 269 kJ (64 Cal)

1 Preheat the oven to 200°C (400°F/ Gas 6). Pierce the eggplants several times with a fork, then cook over an open flame for about 5 minutes, or until the skin is black and blistering. Place in a roasting tin and bake for 40–45 minutes, or until the eggplants are very soft and wrinkled. Cut in half, place in a colander over a bowl to drain off any bitter juices and leave to stand for 30 minutes, or until cool.

2 Carefully peel the skin from the eggplant, chop the flesh and place in a food processor with the garlic, cumin, lemon juice, tahini, cayenne and olive oil. Process until smooth and creamy. Alternatively, use a potato masher or fork. Season with salt and stir in the parsley. Spread onto a flat bowl or plate and garnish with the olives. Serve with pitta bread or pide.

NOTE: *If you prefer, you can simply roast the eggplant in a roasting tin in a 200°C oven for 1 hour, or until very soft and wrinkled. The name baba ghanoush can be roughly translated as 'poor man's caviar'.*

Carefully peel the black and blistered skin away from the baked eggplant.

Process the eggplant, garlic, cumin, lemon juice, tahini, cayenne and olive oil.

Taramasalata

PREPARATION TIME: 10 MINUTES + 10 MINUTES SOAKING | TOTAL COOKING TIME: NIL | SERVES 10

5 slices white bread, crusts removed
80 ml (2½ fl oz/⅓ cup) milk
100 g (3½ oz) tin tarama (mullet roe)
1 egg yolk
½ small onion, grated
1 garlic clove, crushed
2 tablespoons lemon juice
80 ml (2½ fl oz/⅓ cup) olive oil
pinch ground white pepper
pitta bread or pide (Turkish/flat bread),
    to serve

1 Soak the bread in the milk for 10 minutes. Press in a strainer to extract any excess milk, then place in a food processor with the tarama, egg yolk, onion and garlic. Process for 30 seconds, or until smooth, then add 1 tablespoon lemon juice.

2 With the motor running, slowly pour in the olive oil. The mixture should be smooth and of a dipping consistency. Add the remaining lemon juice and a pinch of white pepper. If too salty, add another piece of bread. Serve with pitta bread or pide.

VARIATION: *Try smoked cod's roe instead of the mullet roe.*

NUTRITION PER SERVE
Protein 3.8 g; Fat 10.4 g; Carbohydrate 8.3 g; Dietary Fibre 0.6 g; Cholesterol 57 mg; 596 kJ (142 Cal)

Using a cheese grater, grate half a small onion so that the pieces are small and even.

Press the soaked bread pieces in a strainer to extract any excess milk.

Process the bread, tarama, egg yolk, onion and garlic until smooth.

Pesto

PREPARATION TIME: **10** MINUTES | TOTAL COOKING TIME: **5** MINUTES | SERVES **6**

50 g (1¾ oz) pine nuts
2 very large handfuls small basil leaves
2 garlic cloves, crushed
½ teaspoon sea salt
125 ml (4 fl oz/½ cup) olive oil
30 g (1 oz) finely grated parmesan cheese
20 g (¾ oz) finely grated pecorino cheese
crusty bread, thinly sliced, to serve

1   Preheat the oven to 180°C (350°F/Gas 4).
Spread the pine nuts on a baking tray and bake
for 2 minutes, or until lightly golden. Cool.

2   Process the pine nuts, basil, garlic, salt
and oil in a food processor until smooth.
Transfer to a bowl and stir in the cheeses.
Serve with crusty bread.

NUTRITION PER SERVE
Protein 4 g; Fat 28 g; Carbohydrate 0.5 g; Dietary
Fibre 0.6 g; Cholesterol 7.6 mg; 1118 kJ (267 Cal)

Spread the pine nuts on a baking tray and toast until lightly golden.

Process the pine nuts, basil, garlic, sea salt and oil until smooth.

Transfer to a bowl and stir the parmesan and pecorino into the basil mixture.

Tapenade

PREPARATION TIME: 10 MINUTES | TOTAL COOKING TIME: NIL | SERVES 10

400 g (14 oz) kalamata olives, pitted
2 garlic cloves, crushed
2 anchovy fillets in oil, drained
2 tablespoons capers in brine, rinsed,
    squeezed dry
2 teaspoons chopped thyme
2 teaspoons dijon mustard
1 tablespoon lemon juice
3 tablespoons olive oil
1 tablespoon brandy, optional
crusty bread, thinly sliced, to serve

1 Place the kalamata olives, crushed garlic, anchovies, capers, chopped thyme, dijon mustard, lemon juice, olive oil and brandy, if using, in a food processor and process until smooth. Season with salt and freshly ground black pepper. Spoon into a sterilised jar, cover with a layer of olive oil, seal and refrigerate for up to 1 week. Serve with crusty bread.

NOTE: *When refrigerated, the olive oil may solidify, turning it opaque white. This is a property of olive oil and will not affect the flavour of the dish. Simply bring to room temperature before serving and the olive oil will return to a liquid state. The word 'tapenade' comes from the French word tapéno, meaning caper. Tapenade is the famous olive, anchovy and caper spread from Provence.*

HINT: *To sterilise a storage jar preheat the oven to 120°C (235°F/Gas ½). Wash the jar and lid thoroughly in hot water (preferably in a dishwasher) and dry completely in the warm oven. Do not dry the jar or lid with a tea towel (dish towel).*

NUTRITION PER SERVE
Protein 1.3 g; Fat 2.4 g; Carbohydrate 2 g; Dietary Fibre 8.5 g; Cholesterol 0.6 mg; 376 kJ (90 Cal)

Use an olive pitter or small sharp knife to remove the stones from the olives.

Process all the ingredients (except the bread) in a food processor until smooth.

Burgers, skewers and sausages

Classic burger with barbecue sauce

PREPARATION TIME: 20 MINUTES + 30 MINUTES REFRIGERATION | TOTAL COOKING TIME: 25 MINUTES | SERVES 6

750 g (1 lb 10 oz) minced (ground) beef
250 g (9 oz) minced (ground) sausage
1 small onion, finely chopped
1 tablespoon worcestershire sauce
2 tablespoons tomato sauce (ketchup)
80 g (2¾ oz/1 cup) fresh breadcrumbs
1 egg, lightly beaten
2 large onions, extra, thinly sliced
6 wholemeal (whole-wheat) rolls
6 small lettuce leaves
1 large tomato, sliced

BARBECUE SAUCE
2 teaspoons oil
1 small onion, finely chopped
3 teaspoons brown vinegar
1 tablespoon soft brown sugar
4 tablespoons tomato sauce (ketchup)
2 teaspoons worcestershire sauce
2 teaspoons soy sauce

1   Place the minced beef and sausage in a large bowl. Add the onion, sauces, breadcrumbs and egg. Mix thoroughly with your hands. Divide the mixture into six equal portions and shape into patties. Refrigerate the patties for at least 30 minutes.

2   Place the patties on a hot, lightly oiled barbecue grill plate or flat plate. Barbecue over the hottest part of the fire for 8 minutes each side. Meanwhile, fry the extra onions on an oiled hotplate until golden.

3   To make the barbecue sauce, heat the oil in a small saucepan. Cook the onion for 5 minutes, or until soft. Add the vinegar, sugar and sauces and stir until the sauce comes to the boil. Reduce the heat and simmer for 3 minutes. Allow to cool.

4   Split the rolls in half and fill each one with a lettuce leaf, patty, tomato slice and fried onions. Top with a generous quantity of barbecue sauce.

STORAGE TIME: *Burgers can be prepared up to 4 hours in advance and stored, covered, in the refrigerator. Sauce can be made up to 1 week in advance. Store in the refrigerator.*

NUTRITION PER SERVE
Protein 45 g; Fat 35 g; Carbohydrate 65 g; Dietary Fibre 9 g; Cholesterol 145 mg; 3160 kJ (755 Cal)

Divide the mixture into six portions and shape each into a patty.

Cook the burgers over the hottest part of the fire for 8 minutes on each side.

Beef kebabs with mint yoghurt dressing

PREPARATION TIME: 30 MINUTES + 2 HOURS MARINATING | TOTAL COOKING TIME: 10 MINUTES | MAKES 8 KEBABS

500 g (1 lb 2 oz) lean beef fillet, cubed
125 ml (4 fl oz/½ cup) olive oil
4 tablespoons lemon juice
1 tablespoon chopped rosemary
1 red onion, cut into wedges
200 g (7 oz) slender eggplants (aubergines),
    sliced diagonally

MINT YOGHURT DRESSING
250 g (9 oz/1 cup) plain yoghurt
1 garlic clove, crushed
1 small Lebanese (short) cucumber, grated
2 tablespoons chopped mint

1 Soak 8 wooden skewers in cold water for 30 minutes to prevent scorching. Put the beef in a non-metallic bowl, combine the olive oil, lemon juice and rosemary and pour over the beef. Cover and refrigerate for 2 hours.

2 To make the mint yoghurt dressing, mix together the yoghurt, garlic, cucumber and mint and season with salt and pepper.

3 Drain the beef and discard the marinade. Thread the beef onto the skewers, alternating pieces of beef with the onion wedges and slices of eggplant.

4 Cook the kebabs on a hot, lightly oiled barbecue grill plate or flat plate, turning often, for 5–10 minutes, or until the beef is cooked through and tender. Serve with the dressing.

Marinate the beef in a non-metallic bowl so the acidic marinade doesn't react with the metal.

Alternate cubes of beef with pieces of eggplant and wedges of onion.

NUTRITION PER KEBAB
Protein 15 g; Fat 15 g; Carbohydrate 3 g; Dietary
Fibre 1 g; Cholesterol 40 mg; 1010 kJ (240 Cal)

Pork sausages with herbs

PREPARATION TIME: 10 MINUTES + AT LEAST 3 HOURS MARINATING | TOTAL COOKING TIME: 8–10 MINUTES | MAKES 8 SAUSAGES

8 pork sausages (58 g/2¼ oz each)

HERB MARINADE
3 tablespoons olive oil
2–3 tablespoons lemon juice or balsamic
    vinegar
1–2 garlic cloves, crushed
3 teaspoons soft brown sugar
4 tablespoons chopped mixed herbs—chives,
    lemon thyme, rosemary, parsley, basil,
    coriander (cilantro), mint, oregano and/
    or marjoram

1 Combine the marinade ingredients in a bowl. Season well.

2 Prick the sausages all over and marinate, covered in a non-metallic dish, for at least 3 hours or overnight in the refrigerator.

3 Preheat a barbecue grill plate or flat plate to medium. Drain the sausages, discarding the marinade. Fry the sausages for about 8–10 minutes, or until cooked through, turning during cooking.

Combine the olive oil, lemon juice, crushed garlic, sugar and mixed herbs.

Pour the marinade over the sausages and leave for at least 3 hours.

NUTRITION PER SAUSAGE
Protein 7.1 g; Fat 19.3 g; Carbohydrate 3.3 g; Dietary
Fibre 0.9 g; Cholesterol 38 mg; 898 kJ (214 Cal)

Brunch burger with the works

PREPARATION TIME: 40 MINUTES | TOTAL COOKING TIME: 15 MINUTES | SERVES 6

750 g (1 lb 10 oz) lean minced (ground) beef
1 onion, finely chopped
7 eggs
40 g (1½ oz/½ cup) fresh breadcrumbs
2 tablespoons tomato paste
  (concentrated purée)
1 tablespoon worcestershire sauce
2 tablespoons chopped parsley
3 large onions
30 g (1 oz) butter, plus extra for frying
oil, for brushing
6 slices cheddar cheese
6 bacon slices
6 large hamburger buns, lightly toasted
shredded lettuce
2 tomatoes, thinly sliced
6 large slices beetroot (beets), drained
6 pineapple rings, drained
tomato sauce (ketchup)

1 Mix together the minced beef, onion, 1 egg, breadcrumbs, tomato paste, worcestershire sauce and parsley with your hands. Season well. Divide into six portions and shape into burgers. Cover and set aside.

2 Slice the onions into thin rings. Heat the butter on a barbecue grill plate or flat plate. Cook the onions, turning often, until well browned. Move the onions to the outer edge of the hotplate to keep warm. Brush the hotplate liberally with oil.

3 Cook the burgers for 3–4 minutes each side, or until browned and cooked through. Move to the cooler part of the barbecue or transfer to a plate and keep warm. Place a slice of cheese on each burger.

4 Heat a small amount of butter in a large frying pan. Fry the 6 eggs and bacon until the eggs are cooked through and the bacon is golden and crisp. Fill the hamburger buns with lettuce, tomato, beetroot and pineapple topped with a burger. Pile the onions, egg, bacon and tomato sauce on top of the burger.

NUTRITION PER SERVE
Protein 35 g; Fat 23 g; Carbohydrate 11 g; Dietary Fibre 2 g; Cholesterol 300 mg; 1610 kJ (385 Cal)

Mix together the minced beef, onion, egg, breadcrumbs, tomato paste, sauce and parsley.

Divide the meat mixture into six portions and shape each one into a burger.

Cook the burgers on a barbecue grill plate or flat plate for 3–4 minutes on each side.

Mediterranean chicken skewers

PREPARATION TIME: 20 MINUTES + AT LEAST 2 HOURS MARINATING I TOTAL COOKING TIME: 10 MINUTES I MAKES 8 SKEWERS

32 chicken tenderloins (underbreast fillets)
24 cherry tomatoes
6 button mushrooms, cut into quarters
2 garlic cloves, crushed
grated zest of 1 lemon
2 tablespoons lemon juice
2 tablespoons olive oil
1 tablespoon chopped oregano

1 Soak 8 wooden skewers in cold water for 30 minutes to prevent scorching. Thread a piece of chicken onto each skewer, followed by a tomato, then a piece of mushroom. Repeat three times for each skewer. Finish each skewer with a piece of chicken. Put the skewers in a shallow, non-metallic dish.

2 Combine the garlic, zest, juice, olive oil and chopped oregano, pour over the skewers and toss well. Marinate for at least 2 hours, or overnight if time permits, covered, in the refrigerator.

3 Drain the skewers, reserving the marinade. Cook the skewers on a hot, lightly oiled barbecue grill plate or flat plate for 4 minutes on each side, basting occasionally with the reserved marinade, until the chicken is cooked through and the tomatoes have shrivelled slightly.

NUTRITION PER SKEWER
Protein 34 g; Fat 8 g; Carbohydrate 1 g; Dietary Fibre 1 g; Cholesterol 75 mg; 909 kJ (217 Cal)

Thread the chicken tenderloins, cherry tomatoes and pieces of mushroom onto the skewers.

Put the skewers in a shallow, non-metallic dish and marinate for at least 2 hours.

Cook the skewers for 4 minutes on each side, basting occasionally.

Chicken burgers with tarragon mayonnaise

PREPARATION TIME: 25 MINUTES I TOTAL COOKING TIME: 15 MINUTES I SERVES 6

1 kg (2 lb 4 oz) minced (ground) chicken
1 small onion, finely chopped
2 teaspoons finely grated lemon zest
2 tablespoons sour cream
80 g (2¾ oz/1 cup) fresh breadcrumbs
6 bread rolls
ripe tomato, sliced
handful rocket (arugula) leaves

TARRAGON MAYONNAISE
1 egg yolk
1 tablespoon tarragon vinegar
½ teaspoon French mustard
250 ml (9 fl oz/1 cup) olive oil
white pepper

1 Mix together the minced chicken, onion, zest, sour cream and breadcrumbs with your hands. Divide into six portions and shape into burgers.

2 To make the mayonnaise, put the yolk, half the vinegar and the mustard in a small bowl. Whisk for 1 minute, or until light and creamy. Add the oil about 1 teaspoon at a time, whisking constantly until the mixture thickens. Increase the flow of oil to a thin stream and continue whisking until it has all been incorporated. Stir in the remaining vinegar and season well with salt and white pepper.

3 Cook the burgers on a hot, lightly oiled barbecue grill plate or flat plate for 7 minutes each side, turning once. Serve on a roll with the sliced tomato, rocket and mayonnaise.

NUTRITION PER SERVE
Protein 49 g; Fat 50 g; Carbohydrate 54 g; Dietary Fibre 4 g; Cholesterol 122 mg; 3600 kJ (860 Cal)

The easiest way to mix all the burger ingredients thoroughly is to use your hands.

Add the oil a teaspoon at a time until the mayonnaise thickens, then pour in a thin stream.

Lamb satay sticks with chilli peanut sauce

PREPARATION TIME: 25 MINUTES + 1 HOUR MARINATING | TOTAL COOKING TIME: 15 MINUTES | SERVES 4

600 g (1 lb 5 oz) lamb fillet
2 garlic cloves, crushed
1½ tablespoons finely chopped lemongrass, white part only
2 tablespoons soy sauce
2 teaspoons sugar
¼ teaspoon ground turmeric

CHILLI PEANUT SAUCE
250 g (9 oz/1½ cups) unsalted roasted peanuts
2 tablespoons vegetable oil
1 onion, roughly chopped
1 garlic clove, roughly chopped
1 tablespoon sambal oelek (South-East Asian chilli paste)
1 tablespoon soft brown sugar
1 tablespoon kecap manis or soy sauce (see NOTE)
1 teaspoon grated fresh ginger
1½ teaspoons ground coriander
250 ml (9 fl oz/1 cup) coconut cream
¼ teaspoon ground turmeric

1 Trim the lamb, cut into thin strips and thread onto 8 skewers, bunching along three-quarters of the length. Place in a shallow non-metallic dish. Mix together the garlic, ½ teaspoon freshly ground black pepper, lemongrass, soy sauce, sugar and turmeric and brush over the meat. Leave to marinate for 1 hour.

2 To make the chilli peanut sauce, roughly grind the peanuts in a food processor for 10 seconds. Heat the oil in a small frying pan. Add the onion and garlic and cook over medium heat for 3–4 minutes, or until translucent. Add the sambal oelek, sugar, kecap manis, ginger and coriander. Cook, stirring, for 2 minutes. Add the coconut cream, turmeric and ground peanuts. Reduce the heat and cook for 3 minutes, or until thickened. Season well and then process for 20 seconds, or until the sauce is almost smooth.

3 Drain the skewers, discarding the marinade. Cook the skewers on a hot, lightly oiled barbecue grill plate or flat plate for 2–3 minutes on each side. Serve with the sauce.

NOTE: *Kecap manis is a thick, sweet soy sauce. If you can't find it, use regular soy sauce mixed with a little soft brown sugar.*

NUTRITION PER SERVE
Protein 51 g; Fat 57 g; Carbohydrate 16 g; Dietary Fibre 7 g; Cholesterol 99 mg; 3241 kJ (774 Cal)

Thread the strips of lamb onto the skewers and then marinate for 1 hour.

Coarsely grind the peanuts in a processor and then heat with the other sauce ingredients.

Process the sauce until it is almost smooth and then serve with the skewers.

Tuna skewers with Moroccan spices and chermoula

PREPARATION TIME: 20 MINUTES + 10 MINUTES MARINATING | TOTAL COOKING TIME: 5 MINUTES | SERVES 4

800 g (1 lb 12 oz) tuna steaks, cubed
2 tablespoons olive oil
½ teaspoon ground cumin
2 teaspoons grated lemon zest

CHERMOULA
3 teaspoons ground cumin
½ teaspoon ground coriander
2 teaspoons paprika
pinch of cayenne pepper
4 garlic cloves, crushed
1 large handful flat-leaf (Italian)
    parsley, chopped
2 large handfuls coriander (cilantro), chopped
4 tablespoons lemon juice
125 ml (4 fl oz/½ cup) olive oil
couscous, to serve

1   If using wooden skewers, soak 8 in cold water for 30 minutes beforehand to prevent scorching. Place the tuna in a shallow non-metallic dish. Combine the olive oil, ground cumin and lemon zest and pour over the tuna. Toss to coat and leave to marinate for 10 minutes.

2   To make the chermoula, place the cumin, coriander, paprika and cayenne in a frying pan and cook over medium heat for 30 seconds, or until fragrant. Combine in a small bowl with the remaining ingredients and leave for about 10 minutes so that the flavours develop.

3   Drain the tuna, discarding the marinade. Thread the tuna onto the skewers. Cook on a hot, lightly oiled barbecue grill plate or flat plate until cooked to your taste. Serve on couscous with the chermoula drizzled over the skewers.

Pour the combined olive oil, cumin and lemon zest over the tuna cubes.

Combine the chermoula ingredients in a small bowl and leave for the flavours to develop.

NUTRITION PER SERVE
Protein 50 g; Fat 40 g; Carbohydrate 0 g; Dietary Fibre 0 g; Cholesterol 70 mg; 2186 kJ (520 Cal)

Sweet and sour pork kebabs

PREPARATION TIME: 30 MINUTES + AT LEAST 3 HOURS MARINATING | TOTAL COOKING TIME: 20 MINUTES | SERVES 6

1 kg (2 lb 4 oz) pork fillets, cubed
1 large red capsicum (pepper), cubed
1 large green capsicum (pepper), cubed
425 g (15 oz) tinned pineapple pieces,
    drained, juice reserved
250 ml (9 fl oz/1 cup) orange juice
3 tablespoons white vinegar
2 tablespoons soft brown sugar
2 teaspoons chilli garlic sauce
2 teaspoons cornflour (cornstarch)

1 Soak 12 wooden skewers in cold water for 30 minutes to prevent scorching. Thread pieces of pork alternately with pieces of capsicum and pineapple onto the skewers. Mix the pineapple juice with the orange juice, vinegar, sugar and sauce. Place the kebabs in a shallow non-metallic dish and pour half the marinade over them. Cover and refrigerate for at least 3 hours, turning occasionally.

2 Put the remaining marinade in a small saucepan. Mix the cornflour with a tablespoon of the marinade until smooth, then add to the pan. Stir over medium heat until the mixture boils and thickens. Transfer to a bowl, cover the surface with plastic wrap and leave to cool.

3 Drain the kebabs, discarding the marinade. Cook the kebabs on a hot, lightly oiled barbecue grill plate or flat plate for 15 minutes, turning occasionally, until tender. Serve with the sauce.

Thread pieces of pork onto the skewers, alternating with capsicum and pineapple.

Mix the cornflour with a little of the marinade and then add to the sauce to thicken.

NUTRITION PER SERVE
Protein 40 g; Fat 3 g; Carbohydrate 18 g; Dietary Fibre 2 g; Cholesterol 82 mg; 1073 kJ (256 Cal)

Mushroom and eggplant skewers with tomato sauce

PREPARATION TIME: 20 MINUTES + 15 MINUTES MARINATING I TOTAL COOKING TIME: 30 MINUTES I SERVES 4

12 long rosemary sprigs
18 Swiss brown mushrooms, halved
1 small eggplant (aubergine), cubed
3 tablespoons olive oil
2 tablespoons balsamic vinegar
2 garlic cloves, crushed
1 teaspoon sugar

TOMATO SAUCE
5 tomatoes
1 tablespoon olive oil
1 small onion, finely chopped
1 garlic clove, crushed
1 tablespoon tomato paste
    (concentrated purée)
2 teaspoons sugar
2 teaspoons balsamic vinegar
1 tablespoon chopped flat-leaf
    (Italian) parsley

1   Remove the leaves from the lower part of the rosemary sprigs. Reserve a tablespoon of the leaves. Put the mushrooms and eggplant in a large non-metallic bowl. Pour on the combined oil, vinegar, garlic and sugar and toss to coat. Marinate for 15 minutes.

2   To make the tomato sauce, score a cross in the base of each tomato. Put in a bowl of boiling water for 30 seconds, then plunge into cold water. Peel the skin away from the cross. Cut in half and scoop out the seeds with a teaspoon. Dice the flesh.

3   Heat the oil in a saucepan. Cook the onion and garlic over medium heat for 2–3 minutes, or until soft. Reduce the heat, add the tomato, tomato paste, sugar, vinegar and parsley and simmer for 10 minutes, or until thick.

4   Drain the eggplant and mushrooms, discarding the marinade. Thread alternating mushroom halves and eggplant cubes onto the rosemary sprigs. Cook on a hot, lightly oiled barbecue grill plate or flat plate for 7–8 minutes, or until the eggplant is tender, turning occasionally. Serve with the sauce. Chop the reserved tablespoon of rosemary leaves and sprinkle over the skewers.

NUTRITION PER SERVE
Protein 3 g; Fat 24 g; Carbohydrate 8.5 g; Dietary Fibre 4 g; Cholesterol 0 mg; 1100 kJ (263 Cal)

Simmer the tomato sauce until the liquid has evaporated and the sauce is thick.

Thread alternating cubes of mushrooms and eggplant onto the sprigs.

Beef satay sticks with peanut sauce

PREPARATION TIME: 30 MINUTES + AT LEAST 3 HOURS MARINATING | TOTAL COOKING TIME: 15 MINUTES | SERVES 4

800 g (1 lb 12 oz) rump steak
80 ml (2½ fl oz/⅓ cup) soy sauce
2 tablespoons oil
2 garlic cloves, crushed
1 teaspoon grated fresh ginger

PEANUT SAUCE
250 ml (9 fl oz/1 cup) pineapple juice
250 g (9 oz/1 cup) smooth peanut butter
½ teaspoon garlic powder
½ teaspoon onion powder
2 tablespoons sweet chilli sauce
3 tablespoons soy sauce

1 Trim the steak of excess fat and sinew. Slice across the grain evenly into long, thin strips. Thread onto 8 skewers, bunching them thickly along three-quarters of the skewer. Place in a shallow non-metalic dish.

2 Mix the soy sauce, oil, garlic and ginger together and pour over the skewers. Cover with plastic wrap and refrigerate for several hours or overnight, turning occasionally.

3 Drain the skewers, discarding the marinade. Cook on a hot, lightly oiled barbecue grill plate or flat plate for 8–10 minutes, or until tender, turning the skewers occasionally.

4 To make the peanut sauce, combine the juice, peanut butter, garlic and onion powders and sauces in a small saucepan and stir over medium heat for 5 minutes, or until smooth. Serve warm with the satay sticks.

Trim the meat and then slice across the grain into long, thin strips.

To make the peanut sauce, stir all the ingredients over medium heat until smooth.

NUTRITION PER SERVE
Protein 70 g; Fat 55 g; Carbohydrate 17 g; Dietary Fibre 9 g; Cholesterol 134 mg; 3500 kJ (838 Cal)

Chicken sausages with honey and chilli marinade

PREPARATION TIME: 8 MINUTES + AT LEAST 3 HOURS MARINATING | TOTAL COOKING TIME: 8–10 MINUTES | MAKES 8

8 chicken sausages (76 g/2¾ oz each)

HONEY AND CHILLI MARINADE
3 tablespoons soy sauce
1 tablespoon grated fresh ginger
2 teaspoons grated lemon zest
90 g (3¼ oz/¼ cup) honey
1–2 garlic cloves, crushed
1 tablespoon rice wine
3 tablespoons sweet chilli sauce

1 Combine the marinade ingredients in a bowl. Season well.

2 Prick the sausages all over and marinate, covered in a non-metallic dish, for at least 3 hours or overnight in the refrigerator.

3 Drain the sausages, discarding the marinade. Preheat a barbecue grill plate or flat plate to medium. Fry the sausages for about 8–10 minutes, or until cooked through, turning frequently during cooking.

NUTRITION PER SAUSAGE
Protein 9.3 g; Fat 17.3 g; Carbohydrate 13.7 g; Dietary Fibre 2.1 g; Cholesterol 39 mg; 1050 kJ (251 Cal)

Combine the soy sauce, ginger, lemon zest, honey, garlic, rice wine and chilli sauce in a bowl.

Marinate the sausages in a non-metallic dish, for at least 3 hours in the refrigerator.

Vegetarian burgers with coriander garlic cream

PREPARATION TIME: 30 MINUTES | TOTAL COOKING TIME: 20 MINUTES | MAKES 10 BURGERS

250 g (9 oz/1 cup) red lentils
1 tablespoon oil
2 onions, sliced
1 tablespoon tandoori powder
425 g (15 oz) tinned chickpeas, drained
1 tablespoon grated fresh ginger
1 egg
3 tablespoons chopped flat-leaf (Italian)
    parsley
2 tablespoons chopped coriander (cilantro)
180 g (6 oz/2¼ cups) fresh breadcrumbs
plain (all-purpose) flour, for dusting

CORIANDER GARLIC CREAM
125 g (4½ oz/½ cup) sour cream
125 ml (4 fl oz/½ cup) pouring
    (whipping) cream
1 garlic clove, crushed
2 tablespoons chopped coriander (cilantro)
2 tablespoons chopped flat-leaf (Italian)
    parsley

1 Simmer the lentils in a large pan of water for 8 minutes, or until tender. Drain well. Heat the oil in a frying pan and cook the onion until tender. Add the tandoori powder and stir until fragrant.

2 Put the chickpeas, half the lentils, the ginger, egg and onion mixture in a food processor. Process for 20 seconds, or until smooth. Transfer to a bowl. Stir in the remaining lentils, parsley, coriander and breadcrumbs.

3 Divide the mixture into 10 portions and shape into burgers. (If the mixture is too soft, refrigerate for 15 minutes to firm.) Toss the burgers in flour and place on a hot, lightly oiled barbecue grill plate or flat plate. Cook for 3–4 minutes on each side, or until browned.

4 For the coriander garlic cream, mix together the sour cream, cream, garlic and herbs. Serve with the burgers.

STORAGE: *The burgers can be prepared up to 2 days in advance and stored, covered, in the fridge. The cream can be stored, covered, in the fridge for up to 3 days.*

NOTE: *The coriander garlic cream is also delicious with chicken or fish burgers.*

NUTRITION PER BURGER
Protein 11 g; Fat 14 g; Carbohydrate 26 g; Dietary Fibre 5 g; Cholesterol 50 mg; 1155 kJ (276 Cal)

Heat the oil in a pan and cook the onion until tender, then add the tandoori powder.

Process the chickpea mixture, then transfer to a bowl and mix with the other ingredients.

Shape the portions into burgers and then toss in flour, shaking off the excess, before cooking.

Sesame chicken kebabs

PREPARATION TIME: 10 MINUTES + AT LEAST 2 HOURS MARINATING | TOTAL COOKING TIME: 10 MINUTES | SERVES 4

3 tablespoons oil
2 tablespoons soy sauce
2 tablespoons honey
1 tablespoon grated fresh ginger
1 tablespoon sesame oil
4 large boneless, skinless chicken breasts, cubed
8 spring onions (scallions), cut into short lengths
1 tablespoon sesame seeds, toasted (see HINT)

1 Soak 12 wooden skewers in cold water for 30 minutes to prevent scorching. To make the marinade, whisk together the oil, soy sauce, honey, ginger and sesame oil. Thread the chicken and spring onion alternately onto the skewers and put in a non-metallic dish. Add the marinade, cover and refrigerate for at least 2 hours.

2 Drain the skewers, reserving the marinade. Place the skewers on a hot, lightly oiled barbecue grill plate or flat plate and baste with the remaining marinade. Cook for 4 minutes on each side, or until the chicken is cooked through. Sprinkle with the sesame seeds.

HINT: *To toast sesame seeds, place in a dry pan and shake over moderate heat until golden.*

Thread the pieces of chicken and spring onion alternately onto the skewers.

Once the kebabs are cooked through, sprinkle with the sesame seeds to serve.

NUTRITION PER SERVE
Protein 55 g; Fat 25 g; Carbohydrate 13 g; Dietary Fibre 1 g; Cholesterol 120 mg; 2180 kJ (520 Cal)

Pork sausage burgers with mustard cream

PREPARATION TIME: 20 MINUTES | TOTAL COOKING TIME: 10 MINUTES | SERVES 6

1 kg (2 lb 4 oz) minced (ground) pork
1 small onion, finely chopped
80 g (2¾ oz/1 cup) fresh breadcrumbs
2 garlic cloves, crushed
1 egg, lightly beaten
1 teaspoon dried sage
6 long bread rolls
snow pea (mangetout) sprouts, to serve

MUSTARD CREAM
125 g (4½ oz/½ cup) sour cream
1 tablespoon wholegrain mustard
2 teaspoons lemon juice

1 Mix together the pork, onion, breadcrumbs, garlic, egg and sage with your hands. Divide into six portions and shape into sausages.

2 Cook the sausages on a hot, lightly oiled barbecue grill plate or flat plate for 5–10 minutes, or until cooked through, turning occasionally.

3 To make the mustard cream, put the sour cream, mustard and juice in a small bowl and stir together. Sandwich the sausage burgers in the bread rolls and serve with the mustard cream and snow pea sprouts.

NUTRITION PER SERVE
Protein 51 g; Fat 15 g; Carbohydrate 55 g; Dietary Fibre 4 g; Cholesterol 140 mg; 2342 kJ (559 Cal)

Divide the mixture into six portions and shape each one into a sausage.

Cook the sausages on a hot, lightly oiled barbecue grill plate or flat plate.

Stir together the sour cream, mustard and lemon juice and serve with the burgers.

Vegetable and tofu kebabs

PREPARATION TIME: 40 MINUTES + 30 MINUTES MARINATING | TOTAL COOKING TIME: 30 MINUTES | SERVES 4

500 g (1 lb 2 oz) firm tofu, cubed
1 red capsicum (pepper), cubed
3 zucchini (courgettes), thickly sliced
4 small onions, cut into quarters
300 g (10½ oz) button mushrooms, cut into quarters
125 ml (4 fl oz/½ cup) tamari
125 ml (4 fl oz/½ cup) sesame oil
2.5 cm (1 inch) piece fresh ginger, peeled and grated
180 g (6 oz/½ cup) honey

PEANUT SAUCE
1 tablespoon sesame oil
1 small onion, finely chopped
1 garlic clove, crushed
2 teaspoons chilli paste
250 g (9 oz/1 cup) smooth peanut butter
250 ml (9 fl oz/1 cup) coconut milk
1 tablespoon soft brown sugar
1 tablespoon tamari
1 tablespoon lemon juice
3 tablespoons peanuts, roasted and chopped

1   Preheat the oven to 220°C (425°F/Gas 7). Soak 12 bamboo skewers in cold water for 30 minutes to prevent scorching. Thread the tofu, capsicum, zucchini, onion and mushrooms onto the skewers. Arrange in a shallow, non-metallic dish.

2   Combine the tamari, sesame oil, ginger and honey and pour over the kebabs. Leave to marinate for 30 minutes.

3   To make the peanut sauce, heat the sesame oil in a large frying pan over medium heat and cook the onion, garlic and chilli paste for 1–2 minutes, or until the onion is soft. Reduce the heat, add the peanut butter, coconut milk, sugar, tamari and lemon juice and stir. Bring to the boil, then reduce the heat and simmer for 10 minutes, or until just thick. Stir in the peanuts. If the sauce is too thick, add water.

4   Drain the kebabs, reserving the marinade. Cook the kebabs on a hot, lightly oiled barbecue grill plate or flat plate, basting with the marinade and turning occasionally, for 10–15 minutes, or until tender. Drizzle the peanut sauce over the kebabs and serve.

NUTRITION PER SERVE
Protein 31.5 g; Fat 65 g; Carbohydrate 25.5 g; Dietary Fibre 15 g; Cholesterol 0 mg; 3334 kJ (795 Cal)

Thread alternating pieces of tofu and vegetables onto the skewers.

Simmer the peanut sauce for 10 minutes, or until just thickened.

Cook the skewers, occasionally turning and basting with the marinade.

Thai meatball skewers

PREPARATION TIME: 25 MINUTES | TOTAL COOKING TIME: 10 MINUTES | SERVES 4

700 g (1 lb 9 oz) minced (ground) beef
6 French shallots (eschalots), finely chopped
6 garlic cloves, chopped
5 cm (2 inch) piece fresh ginger, grated
2 tablespoons green or pink peppercorns,
    crushed
4 teaspoons soy sauce
4 teaspoons fish sauce
4 teaspoons soft brown sugar
lime wedges, to serve

1 Soak small wooden skewers in cold water for 30 minutes to prevent scorching. Chop the minced beef with a cleaver or large knife until it is very fine. Mix together the beef, French shallots, garlic, ginger, peppercorns, soy sauce, fish sauce and brown sugar with your hands until well combined.

2 Using 2 teaspoons of mixture at a time, form into balls. Thread three of the balls onto each of the skewers.

3 Cook the skewers on a hot, lightly oiled barbecue grill plate or flat plate, turning frequently, for 7–8 minutes, or until the meat is cooked through. Serve with the lime wedges.

NUTRITION PER SERVE
Protein 78 g; Fat 10 g; Carbohydrate 4 g; Dietary Fibre 1 g; Cholesterol 55 mg; 728 kJ (174 Cal)

Use a large, sharp knife or a cleaver to chop the minced beef until it is very fine.

Form 2 teaspoonfuls of mixture at a time into small, compact balls.

Cook the skewered meatballs, turning frequently, for 7–8 minutes.

Spicy beef burgers with avocado salsa

PREPARATION TIME: 25 MINUTES | TOTAL COOKING TIME: 10 MINUTES | SERVES 6

1 kg (2 lb 4 oz) minced (ground) beef
1 small onion, finely chopped
3 teaspoons chopped chilli
1 teaspoon ground cumin
2 tablespoons tomato paste
    (concentrated purée)
2 tablespoons chopped coriander (cilantro)
6 bread rolls

AVOCADO SALSA
1 avocado
2 tablespoons lime juice
1 small tomato, chopped
125 g (4½ oz/⅔ cup) tinned corn kernels,
    drained

1   With your hands, mix together the minced beef, onion, chilli, cumin, tomato paste and coriander. Divide into 6 portions and shape into burgers.

2   Cook on a hot, lightly oiled barbecue grill plate or flat plate for 4–5 minutes each side.

3   To make the salsa, dice the avocado and toss with the lime juice. Add the tomato and corn and toss lightly. Sandwich the burgers in the bread rolls and serve with the salsa.

NUTRITION PER SERVE
Protein 44 g; Fat 29 g; Carbohydrate 49 g; Dietary Fibre 5 g; Cholesterol 105 mg; 2649 kJ (633 Cal)

The most thorough way to mix the patty ingredients together is to use your hands.

Cook the burgers on a lightly oiled barbecue grill plate or flat plate, turning once.

Mix together the salsa ingredients; the lime juice will prevent the avocado from browning.

Salmon and prawn kebabs

PREPARATION TIME: 15 MINUTES + AT LEAST 2 HOURS MARINATING | TOTAL COOKING TIME: 20 MINUTES | SERVES 6

4 x 200 g (7 oz) salmon fillets

36 raw prawns (shrimp), peeled, deveined, tails intact

5 cm (2 inch) piece fresh ginger, finely shredded

170 ml (5½ fl oz/⅔ cup) Chinese rice wine

185 ml (6 fl oz/¾ cup) kecap manis (see NOTE, page 30)

½ teaspoon five-spice powder

200 g (7 oz) fresh egg noodles

600 g (1 lb 5 oz/1 bunch) baby bok choy (pak choy), leaves separated

NUTRITION PER SERVE
Protein 50 g; Fat 15 g; Carbohydrate 24 g; Dietary Fibre 5 g; Cholesterol 246 mg; 1856 kJ (440 Cal)

1   Soak wooden skewers in cold water for 30 minutes to prevent scorching. Remove the skin and bones from the salmon and cut it into bite-sized cubes (you should have about 36). Thread three cubes of salmon alternately with three prawns onto each skewer. Lay the skewers in a non-metallic dish.

2   Mix together the ginger, rice wine, kecap manis and five-spice powder. Pour over the skewers, then cover and marinate for at least 2 hours. Turn over a few times to ensure even coating.

3   Drain, reserving the marinade. Cook the skewers in batches on a hot, lightly oiled barbecue grill plate or flat plate for 4–5 minutes each side, or until they are cooked through.

4   Meanwhile, place the noodles in a bowl and cover with boiling water. Leave for 5 minutes, or until tender, then drain and keep warm. Place the reserved marinade in a saucepan and bring to the boil. Reduce the heat, simmer and stir in the bok choy leaves. Cook, covered, for 2 minutes, or until the leaves are just wilted.

5   Top the noodles with the bok choy, then the kebabs. Spoon on the heated marinade, season and serve.

Mix together the marinade ingredients and pour over the skewers.

Cook the skewers in batches on a hot barbecue grill plate or flat plate.

Add the bok choy to the reserved marinade in the pan, cover and cook until wilted.

Lamb souvlaki

PREPARATION TIME: 20 MINUTES + OVERNIGHT MARINATING | TOTAL COOKING TIME: 10 MINUTES | SERVES 4

1 kg (2 lb 4 oz) boned lamb leg, trimmed and
   cut into small cubes
3 tablespoons olive oil
2 teaspoons finely grated lemon zest
4 tablespoons lemon juice
2 teaspoons dried oregano
125 ml (4 fl oz/½ cup) dry white wine
2 large garlic cloves, finely chopped
2 bay leaves
250 g (9 oz/1 cup) Greek-style yoghurt
2 garlic cloves, crushed, extra

1   Place the lamb in a non-metallic dish with
2 tablespoons of the olive oil, the lemon zest
and juice, oregano, wine, garlic and bay leaves.
Season with black pepper and toss to coat. Cover
and refrigerate overnight.

2   Place the yoghurt and extra garlic in a bowl,
mix together well and leave for 30 minutes. If
using wooden skewers, soak 8 in cold water for
30 minutes beforehand to prevent scorching.

3   Drain the lamb and pat dry. Discard the
marinade. Thread onto 8 skewers and cook on
a hot barbecue grill plate or flat plate, brushing
with the remaining oil, for 7–8 minutes, or until
brown on the outside and still a little rare in the
middle. Drizzle with the garlic yoghurt and serve
with warm pitta bread.

Toss the lamb and marinade together in a non-metallic bowl.

Brush the remaining oil over the lamb skewers during cooking.

NUTRITION PER SERVE
Protein 43 g; Fat 20 g; Carbohydrate 4 g; Dietary
Fibre 0 g; Cholesterol 126 mg; 1660 kJ (397 Cal)

Pork and tomato burgers

PREPARATION TIME: 20 MINUTES + 15 MINUTES REFRIGERATION | TOTAL COOKING TIME: 15 MINUTES | SERVES 4

350 g (12 oz) minced (ground) pork and veal
100 g (3½ oz) sun-dried tomatoes, chopped
3 spring onions (scallions), finely chopped
2 tablespoons chopped basil
1 red capsicum (pepper), seeded and sliced
1 tablespoon balsamic vinegar

1   Mix together the minced pork and veal, sun-dried tomato, spring onion and basil. Season well and knead for 2 minutes, or until a little sticky. Form into four burgers and refrigerate for 15 minutes.

2   Mix the capsicum with a little olive oil. Cook on a hot, lightly oiled barbecue grill plate or flat plate, tossing well and drizzling with the balsamic vinegar, until just softened. Set aside.

3   Wipe the barbecue clean and reheat. Brush the burgers with a little olive oil and cook for 4–5 minutes each side, or until browned and cooked through. Serve with the chargrilled capsicum.

NUTRITION PER SERVE
Protein 20 g; Fat 10 g; Carbohydrate 5 g; Dietary Fibre 2 g; Cholesterol 45 mg; 840 kJ (200 Cal)

Cook the capsicum, tossing well and drizzling with balsamic vinegar, until softened.

Clean the barbecue grill plate before you reheat it to cook the burgers.

Brush the burgers with a little oil and cook until they are browned.

Involtini of swordfish

PREPARATION TIME: 30 MINUTES | TOTAL COOKING TIME: 10 MINUTES | SERVES 4

1 kg (2 lb 4 oz) swordfish, skin removed, cut into four 5 cm (2 inch) pieces
3 lemons
4 tablespoons olive oil
1 small onion, chopped
3 garlic cloves, chopped
2 tablespoons chopped capers
2 tablespoons chopped pitted kalamata olives
35 g (1¼ oz/⅓ cup) finely grated parmesan cheese
120 g (4¼ oz/1½ cups) fresh breadcrumbs
2 tablespoons chopped flat-leaf (Italian) parsley
1 egg, lightly beaten
24 fresh bay leaves
2 small onions, extra, quartered and separated into pieces
2 tablespoons lemon juice, extra

NUTRITION PER SERVE
Protein 34 g; Fat 38 g; Carbohydrate 5.5 g; Dietary Fibre 5 g; Cholesterol 193 mg; 2065 kJ (493 Cal)

1 Cut each swordfish piece horizontally into four slices to give you 16 slices. Place each piece between two pieces of plastic wrap and roll gently with a rolling pin to flatten without tearing. Cut each piece in half to give 32 pieces.

2 Peel the lemons with a vegetable peeler. Cut the peel into 24 even pieces. Squeeze the lemons to give 3 tablespoons of juice.

3 Heat 2 tablespoons olive oil in a frying pan, add the onion and garlic and cook over medium heat for 2 minutes. Place in a bowl with the capers, olives, parmesan cheese, breadcrumbs and parsley. Season, add the egg and mix to bind.

4 Divide the stuffing among the fish pieces and, with oiled hands, roll up to form parcels. Thread 4 rolls onto each of 8 skewers, alternating with the bay leaves, lemon peel and extra onion.

5 Mix the remaining oil with the lemon juice in a small bowl. Cook the skewers on a hot barbecue grill plate or flat plate for 3–4 minutes each side, basting with the oil and lemon juice mixture. Serve with a little extra lemon juice drizzled over the top.

Roll the swordfish out between two pieces of plastic wrap.

Roll up the fish pieces and filling with oiled hands to form neat parcels.

Thread the rolls, bay leaves, lemon peel and onion onto skewers.

Meatball skewers with capsicum mayonnaise

PREPARATION TIME: 15–20 MINUTES | TOTAL COOKING TIME: 10 MINUTES | SERVES 6

MEATBALLS
750 g (1 lb 10 oz) lean minced (ground) beef
1 onion, very finely chopped
1 egg, lightly beaten
2 garlic cloves, crushed
2–3 tablespoons fresh breadcrumbs

CAPSICUM MAYONNAISE
1 large red capsicum (pepper)
185 g (6½ oz/¾ cup) whole egg mayonnaise
1–2 cloves garlic
lemon juice

1   Combine the beef, onion, egg, garlic and breadcrumbs in a large bowl. Season well. Use your hands to mix thoroughly. Soak wooden skewers in cold water for 30 minutes to prevent scorching.

2   Wet your hands and roll tablespoons of the minced beef mixture into balls. Thread the meatballs onto the skewers.

3   Cook on a hot, lightly oiled barbecue grill plate or flat plate for about 10 minutes, or until the meat is cooked through. Serve the meatballs with the capsicum mayonnaise.

4   To make the mayonnaise, cut the capsicum in half, remove the seeds and membrane and brush the skin lightly with oil. Grill (broil), skin side up, until the skin blisters and blackens. Cover the capsicum with a tea towel (dish towel) or put in a paper or plastic bag to cool. When cool enough to handle, peel away the skin and place the flesh in a food processor. Add the mayonnaise, garlic, salt, pepper and a squeeze of lemon juice. Process until smooth. You could also add some chopped basil.

Wet your hands and roll the minced beef mixture into balls.

Peel away the blistered and blackened skin from the grilled capsicum.

NUTRITION PER SERVE
Protein 28 g; Fat 35.6 g; Carbohydrate 4.5 g; Dietary Fibre 1 g; Cholesterol 131 mg; 1882 kJ (450 Cal)

Skewered lamb with chilli aïoli

PREPARATION TIME: 25 MINUTES + 3 HOURS MARINATING | TOTAL COOKING TIME: 15 MINUTES | MAKES 12 SKEWERS

1.5 kg (3 lb 5 oz) leg of lamb, boned and
   cubed
125 ml (4 fl oz/½ cup) olive oil
125 ml (4 fl oz/½ cup) lemon juice
2 garlic cloves, crushed
1 tablespoon dijon mustard
1 tablespoon chopped oregano

CHILLI AÏOLI
2–3 small red chillies, seeds and stems
   removed
3 garlic cloves
3 egg yolks
2 tablespoons lemon juice
200 ml (7 fl oz) olive oil

1   Put the lamb in a large, non-metallic bowl.
Add the combined olive oil, lemon juice, garlic,
1 teaspoon cracked black pepper, mustard and
oregano. Toss well, cover and refrigerate for at
least 3 hours.

2   Soak 12 wooden skewers in cold water
for 30 minutes to prevent scorching. Drain
the lamb, reserving the marinade. Thread
the lamb onto the skewers and cook on a
hot, lightly oiled barbecue grill plate or flat
plate until well browned, brushing with the
marinade occasionally.

3   To make the chilli aïoli, chop the chillies and
garlic for 30 seconds in a food processor. Add
½ teaspoon ground black pepper, the egg
yolks and half the lemon juice. With the motor
running, slowly pour in the oil in a fine stream.
Increase the flow as the aïoli thickens. Add the
remaining lemon juice and season to taste. Serve
with the skewered lamb.

NUTRITION PER SKEWER
Protein 22.9 g; Fat 31.4 g; Carbohydrate 0.8 g; Dietary
Fibre 0.4 g; Cholesterol 113 mg; 1573 kJ (376 Cal)

Mix the lamb pieces with the marinade to
thoroughly coat the meat.

Pour the oil in a fine stream into the food
processor with the motor running.

Chicken satay with peanut sauce

PREPARATION TIME: 40 MINUTES + 30 MINUTES MARINATING | TOTAL COOKING TIME: 15–20 MINUTES | MAKES 20 SMALL SKEWERS

600 g (1 lb 5 oz) boneless, skinless chicken thighs, trimmed
1 onion, roughly chopped
2 stems lemongrass (white part only), thinly sliced
4 garlic cloves
2 red chillies, chopped
2 teaspoons ground coriander
1 teaspoon ground cumin
1 tablespoon soy sauce
60 ml (2 fl oz/¼ cup) oil
1 tablespoon soft brown sugar

PEANUT SAUCE
125 g (4½ oz/½ cup) crunchy peanut butter
250 ml (9 fl oz/1 cup) coconut milk
125 ml (4 fl oz/½ cup) water
1–2 tablespoons sweet chilli sauce
1 tablespoon soy sauce
2 teaspoons lemon juice

1   Soak 20 short wooden skewers in cold water for 30 minutes to prevent scorching. Cut the chicken into 20 strips and thread one onto each skewer.

2   Process the onion, lemongrass, garlic, chilli, coriander, cumin, ¼ teaspoon salt and soy sauce in a food processor in short bursts until smooth, adding a little oil to assist the processing. Spread over the chicken, cover and refrigerate for 30 minutes.

3   Stir all the peanut sauce ingredients in a saucepan over low heat until the mixture boils. Remove from the heat. The sauce will thicken on standing.

4   Cook the skewers on a hot, lightly oiled barbecue grill plate or flat plate for 2–3 minutes on each side, sprinkling with a little oil and brown sugar. Serve topped with peanut sauce.

NUTRITION PER SKEWER
Protein 30 g; Fat 35 g; Carbohydrate 9 g; Dietary Fibre 6 g; Cholesterol 55 mg; 1945 kJ (465 Cal)

Thread one chicken strip onto each skewer, flattening it out on the skewer.

The peanut sauce will thicken when it has been left to stand.

During cooking, sprinkle the chicken with oil and brown sugar.

Chicken tikka kebabs

PREPARATION TIME: 10 MINUTES + AT LEAST 2 HOURS MARINATING | TOTAL COOKING TIME: 10 MINUTES | SERVES 4

10 boneless, skinless chicken thighs, cubed
1 red onion, cut into wedges
3 tablespoons tikka paste
125 ml (4 fl oz/½ cup) coconut milk
2 tablespoons lemon juice

1 Soak 8 skewers in cold water for 30 minutes to prevent scorching. Thread 2 pieces of chicken and a wedge of onion alternately along each skewer. Place the skewers in a shallow, non-metallic dish.

2 Combine the tikka paste, coconut milk and lemon juice in a jar with a lid. Season and shake well to combine. Pour the mixture over the skewers and marinate for at least 2 hours, or overnight if time permits.

3 Drain, reserving the marinade. Cook the skewers on a hot, lightly oiled barbecue grill plate or flat plate for 4 minutes on each side, or until the chicken is cooked through. Put any left-over marinade in a small saucepan and bring to the boil. Serve as a sauce with the tikka kebabs.

NUTRITION PER SERVE
Protein 50 g; Fat 13 g; Carbohydrate 4 g; Dietary Fibre 1.5 g; Cholesterol 114 mg; 1457 kJ (350 Cal)

Thread a couple of pieces of chicken and then a wedge of onion and repeat until the skewer is full.

Mix the tikka marinade in a screw-top jar and then pour over the kebabs.

Cook the kebabs on a barbecue grill plate or flat plate until the chicken is cooked through.

Lamb koftas with tahini dressing

PREPARATION TIME: 25 MINUTES | TOTAL COOKING TIME: 10 MINUTES | SERVES 4–6

600 g (1 lb 5 oz) lean lamb
1 onion, roughly chopped
2 garlic cloves, roughly chopped
1½ teaspoons ground cumin
½ teaspoon ground cinnamon
1 teaspoon sweet paprika
2 slices bread, crusts removed
1 egg, lightly beaten
olive oil, for coating

TAHINI DRESSING
2 tablespoons tahini (sesame paste)
3 teaspoons lemon juice
1 garlic clove, crushed
2 tablespoons sour cream
1 tablespoon chopped flat-leaf (Italian) parsley

1 If using wooden skewers, soak them in cold water for 30 minutes to prevent scorching. Trim the meat of any excess fat and sinew. Cut into small pieces and put in a food processor with the remaining ingredients. Add 1 teaspoon cracked black pepper and 1 teaspoon salt. Process until the mixture becomes a smooth paste.

2 Divide the mixture into 12 portions. Shape into sausages around 12 metal skewers.

3 To make the dressing, combine all the ingredients with a pinch of salt and 2–3 tablespoons water and stir until creamy.

4 Arrange the kebabs on a hot, lightly oiled barbecue grill plate or flat plate. Cook for 10 minutes, turning frequently, until browned and cooked through. Serve with the dressing.

NUTRITION PER SERVE (6)
Protein 23 g; Fat 10 g; Carbohydrate 6 g; Dietary Fibre 1 g; Cholesterol 75 mg; 856 kJ (205 Cal)

Mix the kofta ingredients in a food processor until a smooth paste forms.

Shape the kofta mixture into sausages around the skewers.

Cheeseburger with capsicum salsa

PREPARATION TIME: 25 MINUTES + 1 HOUR STANDING | TOTAL COOKING TIME: 20 MINUTES | SERVES 6

1 kg (2 lb 4 oz) minced (ground) beef
1 small onion, finely chopped
2 tablespoons chopped flat-leaf (Italian)
     parsley
1 teaspoon dried oregano
1 tablespoon tomato paste
     (concentrated purée)
70 g (2½ oz) cheddar cheese
6 bread rolls

CAPSICUM SALSA
2 red capsicums (peppers)
1 ripe tomato, finely chopped
1 small red onion, finely chopped
1 tablespoon olive oil
2 teaspoons red wine vinegar

1 Mix together the minced beef, onion, herbs and tomato paste with your hands. Divide into six portions and shape into patties. Cut the cheese into small squares. Make a cavity in the top of each patty with your thumb. Place a piece of cheese in the cavity and smooth the beef over to enclose the cheese completely.

2 To make the salsa, quarter the capsicums, remove the seeds and membranes and cook on a hot, lightly oiled barbecue grill plate or flat plate, skin side down, until the skin blackens and blisters. Place in a plastic bag and leave to cool. Peel away the skin and dice the flesh. Combine with the tomato, onion, olive oil and vinegar and leave for at least 1 hour to let the flavours develop. Serve at room temperature.

3 Cook the patties on a hot, lightly oiled barbecue grill plate or flat plate for 4–5 minutes each side, turning once. Serve in rolls with salad leaves and the capsicum salsa.

STORAGE: *The salsa will keep for a day in the fridge. The burgers can be kept in the fridge for 4 hours before cooking.*

VARIATION: *Camembert, brie or any blue cheese can be used to stuff the burgers.*

NUTRITION PER SERVE
Protein 46 g; Fat 28 g; Carbohydrate 47 g; Dietary Fibre 4 g; Cholesterol 117 mg; 2600 kJ (620 Cal)

Make an indentation in the burger with your thumb, then press a piece of cheese inside.

Cook the capsicum on a hotplate until the skin blackens and will peel away easily.

Cook the burgers on a barbecue grill plate or flat plate for 4–5 minutes on each side.

Chilli beef burgers with mustard butter

PREPARATION TIME: 25 MINUTES + 2 HOURS REFRIGERATION | TOTAL COOKING TIME: 10 MINUTES | MAKES 18 BURGERS

1 kg (2 lb 4 oz) minced (ground) beef
3 onions, grated
3 tablespoons chopped parsley
150 g (5½ oz/1½ cups) dry breadcrumbs
1 egg, lightly beaten
1 tablespoon milk
1 tablespoon malt vinegar
1 tablespoon tomato paste
    (concentrated purée)
2 tablespoons soy sauce
1 tablespoon chilli sauce
3 tablespoons dried oregano

MUSTARD BUTTER
125 g (4½ oz) butter, softened
2 tablespoons sour cream
2 tablespoons German mustard

1 Mix together the beef, onion, parsley, breadcrumbs, egg, milk, vinegar, tomato paste, sauces and oregano. Refrigerate, covered with plastic wrap, for 2 hours.

2 To make the mustard butter, beat the butter, sour cream and mustard in a small bowl for 2 minutes, or until well combined. Leave for 20 minutes to let the flavours develop.

3 Divide the burger mixture into 18 portions and shape each one into a burger. Cook on a hot, lightly oiled barbecue grill plate or flat plate for 4 minutes on each side. Serve immediately with the mustard butter.

Mix together all the burger ingredients and then refrigerate for 2 hours.

Divide the mixture into 18 portions and shape each into a round burger.

NUTRITION PER BURGER
Protein 13 g; Fat 13 g; Carbohydrate 6 g; Dietary Fibre 1 g; Cholesterol 66 mg; 811 kJ (200 Cal)

Teriyaki fish with mango and kiwi salsa

PREPARATION TIME: 30 MINUTES + 30 MINUTES MARINATING | TOTAL COOKING TIME: 10 MINUTES | SERVES 4

750 g (1 lb 10 oz) swordfish fillets, cut into
cubes

MARINADE
125 ml (4 fl oz/½ cup) teriyaki sauce
3 tablespoons pineapple juice
2 tablespoons honey
1 tablespoon grated fresh ginger
2 garlic cloves, crushed
1 teaspoon sesame oil

SALSA
1 red onion, chopped
2 teaspoons sugar
2 tablespoons lime juice
1 firm mango, diced
140 g (5 oz/¾ cup) diced pineapple
1 kiwi fruit, diced
2 small red chillies, seeded and finely chopped
2 tablespoons finely chopped coriander
(cilantro) leaves

1   Soak 8 wooden skewers in cold water for
30 minutes to prevent scorching. Place the cubes
of fish in a non-metallic bowl. Combine the
marinade ingredients, pour over the fish and stir
to coat. Cover and refrigerate for 30 minutes.

2   Drain, reserving the marinade. Thread the
fish onto the skewers.

3   To make the salsa, put the onion in a
bowl and sprinkle with sugar. Add the other
ingredients and mix together gently.

4   Cook the skewers on a hot, lightly oiled
barbecue grill plate or flat plate for 6–8 minutes,
turning often and basting with the reserved
marinade. Serve with the salsa.

NUTRITION PER SERVE
Protein 50 g; Fat 18 g; Carbohydrate 40 g; Dietary
Fibre 3 g; Cholesterol 145 mg; 2153 kJ (515 Cal)

Swordfish is a firm, meaty fish, perfect for
barbecuing. Cut it into cubes.

Sprinkle the onion with sugar and then mix with all
the other salsa ingredients.

Indian seekh kebabs

PREPARATION TIME: 40 MINUTES | TOTAL COOKING TIME: 12 MINUTES | SERVES 4

pinch of ground cloves
pinch of ground nutmeg
½ teaspoon chilli powder
1 teaspoon ground cumin
2 teaspoons ground coriander
3 garlic cloves, finely chopped
5 cm (2 inch) piece fresh ginger, grated
500 g (1 lb 2 oz) lean minced (ground) beef

ONION AND MINT RELISH
1 red onion, finely chopped
1 tablespoon white vinegar
1 tablespoon lemon juice, plus extra
1 tablespoon chopped mint

1   Soak 12 thick wooden skewers in cold water for 30 minutes to prevent scorching. Dry-fry the cloves, nutmeg, chilli, cumin and coriander in a heavy-based frying pan over low heat for 2 minutes, shaking the pan constantly. Transfer to a bowl with the garlic and ginger and set aside.

2   Knead the minced beef firmly with your fingertips and the base of your hand for 3 minutes, or until very soft and a little sticky (this gives the kebabs the correct soft texture when cooked). Add the minced beef to the spice and garlic mixture and mix well, seasoning with plenty of salt and pepper.

3   Form tablespoons of the meat into small, round patties. Wet your hands and press two portions of the meat around a skewer, leaving a small gap at the top. Smooth the outside gently, place on baking paper and refrigerate while making the remaining kebabs.

4   To make the relish, mix the onion, vinegar and lemon juice and refrigerate for 10 minutes. Stir in the mint and season with pepper.

5   Cook the skewers on a hot, lightly oiled barbecue grill plate or flat plate for about 8 minutes, turning regularly and sprinkling with a little lemon juice. Serve with the relish.

NOTE: *These kebabs freeze very well—simply defrost before barbecuing.*

NUTRITION PER SERVE
Protein 16 g; Fat 13 g; Carbohydrate 2 g; Dietary Fibre 1 g; Cholesterol 47 mg; 798 kJ (190 Cal)

Peel and chop the garlic and peel and grate the piece of fresh ginger.

Dry-fry the cloves, nutmeg, chilli, cumin and coriander in a heavy-based pan.

Form the meat mixture into small patties and then press two around each skewer.

Herb burgers

PREPARATION TIME: 20 MINUTES | TOTAL COOKING TIME: 20 MINUTES | MAKES 8 BURGERS

750 g (1 lb 10 oz) minced (ground)
    beef or lamb
2 tablespoons chopped basil
1 tablespoon snipped chives
1 tablespoon chopped rosemary
1 tablespoon chopped thyme
2 tablespoons lemon juice
80 g (2¾ oz/1 cup) fresh breadcrumbs
1 egg
2 baguettes
lettuce leaves
2 tomatoes, sliced
tomato sauce (ketchup)

1 Combine the minced beef or lamb with the herbs, lemon juice, breadcrumbs and egg. Season well with salt and pepper. Mix well with your hands. Divide the mixture into eight portions and shape into thick rectangular patties.

2 Place the burgers on a hot, lightly oiled barbecue grill plate or flat plate. Cook for 5–10 minutes each side until well browned and just cooked through.

3 Cut the baguettes in half and sandwich with the burgers, lettuce, tomato and tomato sauce.

NUTRITION PER BURGER
Protein 26 g; Fat 12 g; Carbohydrate 32 g; Dietary Fibre 2 g; Cholesterol 32 mg; 1455 kJ (350 Cal)

Put the beef or lamb, herbs, juice, breadcrumbs, egg and seasoning in a bowl and mix well.

Shape the mixture into rectangular patties and cook on the grill plate or flat plate for 10–20 minutes.

Make sandwiches from the baguettes, burgers and salad ingredients.

Persian chicken skewers

PREPARATION TIME: 10 MINUTES + OVERNIGHT MARINATING | TOTAL COOKING TIME: 10 MINUTES | SERVES 4

the skewers for 4 minutes on each side, or the chicken is cooked through.

The following is a newspaper clipping overlaid on the page:

bar occupying one wall.

Luckily, there were a few spaces left in the stainless steel and red modern sports bar in the centre of the building, and in a cute, covered courtyard off the restaurant.

We grabbed two menus off the bar and weaved our way through the deep-in-thought trivia crowd to the courtyard.

The menu at Aspley Hotel is modern and inviting.

There are the compulsory steaks, some light entrees, plus a variety of appetising mains like our mimosa prawn risotto and parmesan-crusted lamb cutlets.

We started, though, with a contemporary pub favourite — the salt and pepper calamari.

This was a very good version with a generous serve of tender and nicely seasoned rolls of scored calamari on a bed of simple salad.

Our mains weren't on quite the same level, but were enjoyable

The cutlets came with a bowl of vegies. I don't normally eat vegetables at pubs as I often find them boiled beyond recognition, but this mix of broccoli, cauliflower, carrot and squash was delightfully fresh and just cooked, so it had crunch.

The bar in the restaurant area has less variety than the sports bar. However, a good range of beer is available in both spaces, including the less commonly found Barons Lemon Myrtle and Blue Tongue on tap.

The wine list is simple and fairly standard of most suburban pubs, with well-known labels from popular wineries.

You have to order food and drinks at the bar and are given a buzzer to identify when your meal is ready to be collected. Though this makes service difficult to judge, the meals were ready in good time (especially considering how busy the place was) and the bar staff were efficient.

The Aspley Hotel is a simple, well-packaged venue with a pokies room out the back which has appeal as a local for the suburb's residents.

WHERE Aspley Hotel, 1247 Gympie Rd, Aspley, ph: 3863 0055.

WHEN Mon-Sat 10am-midnight, Sun 10am-10pm.

WHAT Entrees $5.90-$25.90; mains $16.90-$33.90; wine $4.50-$18 per glass, $18-$80 per bottle.

Verdict			
Food	**13**	Service	**13**
Drinks	**13**	Ambience	**13**
All scores are marked out of 20			

Modern and inviting: The prawn risotto as served at Brisbane's Aspley Hotel (top)

thesundaymail.com.au   EV

Left column fragments:

ghtly acidic e, and the ginger and

e and hearty with their

ed ordering which in-n offerings ulfi, as well ake.

value for so serves a anquets for g at $24.90 rees, main, ts.

hout being sounding a Our meals nd the staff

well-priced decorative aroo will hit

vendish Rd, 55.

5.30pm-

90; mains sert

vice	**14**
bience	**15**
ut of 20	

20

NUTRITION PER SERVE
Protein 35 g; Fat 18 g; Carbohydrate 0.5 g; Dietary Fibre 0.5 g; Cholesterol 75 mg; 1259 kJ (300 Cal)

Meat

Pork with apple and onion wedges

PREPARATION TIME: 25 MINUTES | TOTAL COOKING TIME: 15 MINUTES | SERVES 4

2 pork fillets, about 400 g (14 oz) each
12 pitted prunes
2 green apples, unpeeled, cored, cut
    into wedges
2 red onions, cut into wedges
50 g (1¾ oz) butter, melted
2 teaspoons caster (superfine) sugar
125 ml (4 fl oz/½ cup) pouring
    (whipping) cream
2 tablespoons brandy
1 tablespoon snipped chives

NUTRITION PER SERVE
Protein 25 g; Fat 25 g; Carbohydrate 25 g; Dietary
Fibre 4 g; Cholesterol 130 mg; 1920 kJ (455 Cal)

1 Trim the pork of any excess fat and sinew and cut each fillet in half. Make a slit with a knife through the centre of each fillet and push 3 prunes into each one. Brush the pork, the apple and onion wedges with the melted butter and sprinkle the apple and onion with the caster sugar.

2 Brown the pork on a hot, lightly oiled barbecue grill plate or flat plate. Add the apple and onion wedges (you may need to cook in batches if your grill plate or flat plate isn't large enough). Cook, turning frequently, for 5–7 minutes, or until the pork is cooked through and the apple and onion pieces are softened. Remove the pork, apple and onion from the barbecue and keep warm.

3 Mix together the cream, brandy and chives in a frying pan. Transfer to the stove top and simmer for 3 minutes, or until slightly thickened. Season with salt and black pepper.

4 Slice the meat, apple and onion wedges and serve with the brandy cream sauce.

Make a slit through the centre of the pork and fill with three prunes.

Brush the apple and onion with melted butter and then sprinkle with caster sugar.

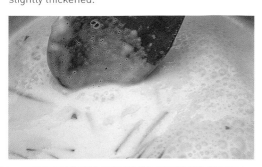
Simmer the brandy cream sauce until it has slightly thickened.

Fillet of beef with mustard coating

PREPARATION TIME: 1 HOUR + 1 HOUR STANDING | TOTAL COOKING TIME: 40 MINUTES | SERVES 8

2 kg (4 lb 8 oz) piece fillet steak
3 tablespoons brandy
4 tablespoons wholegrain mustard
3 tablespoons pouring (whipping) cream

1 Prepare a kettle or covered barbecue for indirect cooking at moderate heat (normal fire); see page 249. Trim the meat of excess fat and sinew and tie securely with string at regular intervals to help it retain its shape. Brush all over with the brandy and leave for 1 hour.

2 Mix together the mustard, cream and ¾ teaspoon of coarsely ground black pepper and spread evenly over the fillet.

3 Place the meat on a large greased sheet of foil. Pinch the corners securely to form a tray to hold in the juices. Cover the barbecue and cook for 30–40 minutes for medium-rare meat. Leave for 10–15 minutes before carving into thick slices. If you like, stir a tablespoon of mustard into the pan juices to make a gravy.

STORAGE: *The beef can be marinated in brandy for up to a day. Keep, covered, in the fridge. Allow to come to room temperature for about 30 minutes before cooking.*

NUTRITION PER SERVE
Protein 54 g; Fat 14 g; Carbohydrate 0 g; Dietary Fibre 0 g; Cholesterol 130 mg; 1480 kJ (350 Cal)

Tie the meat at intervals with string so that it keeps its shape.

Mix together the mustard, cream and pepper and spread over the meat.

Pinch up the corners of the foil to make a tray that will hold the meat juices.

Steak in red wine

PREPARATION TIME: 10 MINUTES + 3 HOURS MARINATING | TOTAL COOKING TIME: 10 MINUTES | SERVES 4

750 g (1 lb 10 oz) rump steak
250 ml (9 fl oz/1 cup) red wine
2 teaspoons garlic salt
1 tablespoon dried oregano

1   Trim the steak of any fat. Mix together the wine, salt and oregano with cracked black pepper to taste. Put the steak in a shallow, non-metallic dish and add the marinade. Toss well, cover and refrigerate for at least 3 hours.

2   Drain, reserving the marinade. Cook the steak on a hot, lightly oiled barbecue grill plate or flat plate for 3–4 minutes on each side, brushing frequently with the marinade.

HINT: *Choose a basting brush with pure bristles. Nylon bristles can melt in the heat of the barbecue.*

NUTRITION PER SERVE
Protein 44 g; Fat 5 g; Carbohydrate 0 g; Dietary
Fibre 0 g; Cholesterol 126 mg; 1100 kJ (264 Cal)

Trim the steak of any excess fat and sinew before marinating.

Mix together the wine, salt, oregano and pepper and pour over the steak.

Cook the steak on a hotplate, brushing frequently with the wine marinade.

Lamb with salsa verde and polenta wedges

PREPARATION TIME: 40 MINUTES + 20 MINUTES | TOTAL COOKING TIME: 35 MINUTES | SERVES 4

SALSA VERDE
2 large handfuls parsley
2 very large handfuls basil
2 large handfuls mint
30 g (1 oz) dill
2 tablespoons capers
1–2 garlic cloves
1 tablespoon caster (superfine) sugar
1 teaspoon grated lemon zest
1 tablespoon lemon juice
1 slice white bread
2–3 anchovy fillets
80 ml (2½ fl oz/⅓ cup) olive oil

POLENTA WEDGES
500 ml (17 fl oz/2 cups) chicken stock
150 g (5½ oz/1 cup) polenta
50 g (1¼ oz) butter
125 ml (4 fl oz/½ cup) pouring
     (whipping) cream

12 lamb cutlets, trimmed

1 To make the salsa verde, chop the herbs, capers, garlic, sugar, lemon zest, juice, bread and anchovies in a food processor. With the motor running, add the oil in a thin stream and blend until smooth.

2 To make the polenta, heat the stock until boiling. Add the polenta, stirring over low heat for 20 minutes until it leaves the side of the pan. Stir in the butter and cream and season. Grease a deep 23 cm (9 inch) round cake tin, spoon in the polenta and smooth the top. Set in the fridge for 20 minutes.

3 Turn out the polenta, cut into wedges and brush with melted butter. Cook on a hot, lightly oiled barbecue grill plate or flat plate for 2–3 minutes each side, or until brown.

4 Cook the lamb for 2 minutes on each side, or until cooked through but still just pink inside. Serve with salsa and wedges.

NUTRITION PER SERVE
Protein 30 g; Fat 50 g; Carbohydrate 35 g; Dietary Fibre 3 g; Cholesterol 150 mg; 2985 kJ (710 Cal)

Trimming the lamb bones of any excess fat or sinew makes them easier to hold.

Finely chop the ingredients for the salsa verde in a food processor.

When the polenta leaves the side of the pan, stir in the butter and cream.

Chilli pork ribs

PREPARATION TIME: 15 MINUTES + OVERNIGHT MARINATING | TOTAL COOKING TIME: 20 MINUTES | SERVES 4–6

1 kg (2 lb 4 oz) pork spare ribs
125 g (4½ oz) tin tomato passata
  (puréed tomatoes)
2 tablespoons honey
2 tablespoons chilli sauce
2 tablespoons hoisin sauce
2 tablespoons lime juice
2 garlic cloves, crushed
1 tablespoon oil

1 Cut each rib into thirds, then lay them in a single layer in a shallow non-metallic dish.

2 Mix together all the other ingredients except the oil and pour over the meat, turning to coat well. Cover with plastic wrap and refrigerate overnight, turning occasionally.

3 Drain the ribs, reserving the marinade, and cook them over medium heat on a lightly oiled barbecue grill plate or flat plate. Baste often with the marinade and cook for 15–20 minutes, or until the ribs are tender and well browned, turning occasionally. Season to taste before serving immediately.

NUTRITION PER SERVE (6)
Protein 15 g; Fat 26 g; Carbohydrate 9 g; Dietary
Fibre 0 g; Cholesterol 90 mg; 1399 kJ (333 Cal)

Use a sharp knife to cut each of the pork ribs into thirds, then place in a shallow dish.

Mix together all the ingredients for the marinade and then pour over the ribs.

Turn the ribs and baste often with the marinade while they are cooking.

Steak with bocconcini, tomato and capsicum salsa

PREPARATION TIME: 20 MINUTES | TOTAL COOKING TIME: 10 MINUTES | SERVES 6

6 fillet steaks (125 g/4½ oz each)

SALSA
180 g (6 oz) bocconcini (fresh baby mozzarella cheese), diced
200 g (7 oz) tomatoes, diced
50 g (1¾ oz/⅓ cup) drained sun-dried capsicum (pepper) in oil, chopped
1 spring onion (scallion), finely sliced
1 tablespoon extra virgin olive oil
2 teaspoons red wine vinegar
1 tablespoon shredded basil
1 tablespoon chopped flat-leaf (Italian) parsley

1 Mix together the bocconcini, tomato, sun-dried capsicum and spring onion in a large bowl.

2 Whisk together the oil and vinegar until thoroughly blended. Stir through the basil and parsley.

3 Cook the steaks on a hot, lightly oiled barbecue grill plate or flat plate for 4–5 minutes each side, turning once.

4 Toss the dressing with the salsa and season well with salt and pepper. Serve at room temperature with the steaks.

NUTRITION PER SERVE
Protein 32.6 g; Fat 14.3 g; Carbohydrate 3.6 g; Dietary Fibre 1.7 g; Cholesterol 94 mg; 1166 kJ (279 Cal)

Mix together the bocconcini, tomato, sun-dried capsicum and spring onion.

Stir the basil and flat-leaf parsley into the vinaigrette dressing.

Moroccan lamb with pistachio couscous

PREPARATION TIME: 40 MINUTES + 2 HOURS MARINATING | TOTAL COOKING TIME: 20 MINUTES | SERVES 4

MOROCCAN MARINADE
3 tablespoons olive oil
1 tablespoon lemon juice
2 teaspoons honey
1–2 garlic cloves, crushed
1 teaspoon ground cumin
½ teaspoon ground turmeric
½ teaspoon ground cinnamon
¼ teaspoon cayenne pepper

8–10 small lamb fillets
pinch of saffron
375 ml (13 fl oz/1½ cups) hot chicken stock
250 g (9 oz/1⅓ cups) couscous
1 tablespoon olive oil
1 red onion, chopped
1 red chilli, seeded and chopped
2 garlic cloves, crushed
75 g (2½ oz/½ cup) currants
100 g (3½ oz) shelled pistachio nuts
grated zest of 1 lemon
grated zest of 1 orange
3 tablespoons chopped mint

1   Mix together all the marinade ingredients. Put the lamb in a shallow, non-metallic dish, add the marinade, cover and refrigerate for 2 hours.

2   Add the saffron to the hot stock and pour over the couscous. Cover and set aside for 10 minutes, then stir to remove lumps.

3   Heat the oil in a frying pan, add the onion, chilli and garlic and cook for 3 minutes. Add the currants and nuts and cook for 5 minutes. Stir in the lemon and orange zest and the mint. Stir through the couscous.

4   Drain the lamb, discarding the marinade. Cook the lamb on a hot, lightly oiled barbecue grill plate or flat plate, turning once, until browned all over. Cook for 2–3 minutes more, turning frequently. Serve with the couscous.

NUTRITION PER SERVE
Protein 45 g; Fat 40 g; Carbohydrate 50 g; Dietary Fibre 5 g; Cholesterol 110 mg; 3030 kJ (720 Cal)

Mix together all the ingredients for the Moroccan marinade and pour over the lamb.

Stir the onion, chilli, garlic, currants, nuts, zest and mint through the couscous.

Cook the lamb on a hotplate until browned all over and then cook for a little longer.

T-bone steak with sweet onions

PREPARATION TIME: 10 MINUTES | TOTAL COOKING TIME: 20 MINUTES | SERVES 4

4 tablespoons oil
6 onions, sliced into rings
3 tablespoons barbecue sauce
4 T-bone steaks

1 Heat 2 tablespoons of the oil on a hot barbecue grill plate or flat plate. Add the onions and barbecue sauce and cook, stirring regularly, for 10 minutes, or until the onions are very soft and brown. Push to one side of the hotplate to keep warm.

2 Brush the T-bone steaks with the remaining oil and add to the hotplate. Cook over high heat, turning once or twice, until tender and cooked to your liking. Arrange the steaks on warm plates, spoon over some of the sweet caramelised onions, and serve.

NUTRITION PER SERVE
Protein 40 g; Fat 30 g; Carbohydrate 15 g; Dietary Fibre 2 g; Cholesterol 85 mg; 1995 kJ (475 Cal)

You will need six onions for this recipe—they reduce in volume once they're caramelised

Cook the onions with the barbecue sauce until they are fully caramelised.

Brush the T-bone steaks with the remaining oil and then cook over high heat.

Ginger-orange pork

PREPARATION TIME: 15 MINUTES + AT LEAST 3 HOURS MARINATING | TOTAL COOKING TIME: 20 MINUTES | SERVES 6

6 pork butterfly steaks (150 g/5½ oz each)
250 ml (9 fl oz/1 cup) ginger wine
150 g (5½ oz/½ cup) orange marmalade
2 tablespoons oil
1 tablespoon grated fresh ginger

1   Trim the pork steaks of excess fat and sinew. Mix together the wine, marmalade, oil and ginger. Place the steaks in a shallow non-metallic dish and add the marinade. Store, covered with plastic wrap, in the fridge for at least 3 hours, turning occasionally. Drain, reserving the marinade.

2   Cook the pork on a hot, lightly oiled barbecue grill plate or flat plate for 5 minutes each side or until tender, turning once.

3   While the meat is cooking, place the reserved marinade in a small saucepan. Bring to the boil, reduce the heat and simmer for 5 minutes, or until the marinade has reduced and thickened slightly. Pour over the pork.

HINT: *Steaks of uneven thickness may curl when cooked. Prevent this by leaving a layer of fat on the outside and making a few deep cuts in it prior to cooking. Remove the fat before serving.*

NUTRITION PER SERVE
Protein 36.9 g; Fat 7 g; Carbohydrate 15.4 g; Dietary Fibre 0.2 g; Cholesterol 81 mg; 1255 kJ (300 Cal)

Put the pork in a shallow non-metallic dish so that the marinade doesn't react with the metal.

Cook the pork on a hotplate for 5 minutes on each side, or until tender.

Place the left-over marinade in a small pan and boil until reduced and thickened to a sauce.

Veal with skordalia and tomato beans

PREPARATION TIME: 45 MINUTES I TOTAL COOKING TIME: 40 MINUTES I SERVES 4

SKORDALIA
350 g (12 oz) potatoes
3 tablespoons toasted blanched almonds
2 garlic cloves
1 tablespoon white wine vinegar
4 tablespoons olive oil

TOMATO BEANS
6 tomatoes, peeled, seeded and chopped
3 garlic cloves, chopped
1 teaspoon caster (superfine) sugar
300 g (10½ oz) tinned cannellini beans
2 large handfuls parsley, chopped

8 veal cutlets
lemon pepper seasoning

1   To make the skordalia, cut the potatoes into large pieces and boil for 15–20 minutes, or until tender. Drain and cool. Finely chop the toasted almonds in a food processor. Peel and mash the potato, then stir in the almonds, garlic and vinegar. Gradually pour in the olive oil, stirring constantly, until all the oil is incorporated. Season well.

2   To make the beans, heat a little olive oil in a heavy-based frying pan and add the tomato, garlic and sugar. Bring to the boil, reduce the heat and simmer, stirring frequently, for 15 minutes, or until thickened. Stir in the rinsed and drained beans and parsley. Season.

3   Trim the veal of fat and sinew and coat liberally with the lemon pepper. Cook on a hot, lightly oiled barbecue grill plate or flat plate for 3 minutes each side, depending on the thickness of the cutlets. Serve with the beans and skordalia.

NUTRITION PER SERVE
Protein 35 g; Fat 25 g; Carbohydrate 35 g; Dietary
Fibre 5 g; Cholesterol 85 mg; 2200 kJ (525 Cal)

Peel the cooked potatoes, then mash with a potato masher.

Mix the beans, parsley and salt and pepper into the tomatoes.

Trim the veal cutlets of any excess fat and sinew before they are barbecued.

Pork with sun-dried tomato and basil butter

PREPARATION TIME: 15 MINUTES I TOTAL COOKING TIME: 5–7 MINUTES I SERVES 4

SUN-DRIED TOMATO AND
BASIL BUTTER
125 g (4½ oz) butter
30 g (1 oz) finely chopped sun-dried tomatoes
    packed in oil
1 tablespoon finely shredded basil
20 g (¾ oz) finely grated parmesan cheese

2 pork fillets (400 g/14 oz each)

1 Beat the butter until light and creamy, then drain and add the tomatoes, basil and parmesan cheese and mix together well. Spoon the butter into small pots and swirl the surface with a flat-bladed knife.

2 Trim the pork of any excess fat and sinew and cut each fillet in half. Cook the pork on a hot, lightly oiled barbecue grill plate or flat plate, turning frequently, for 5–7 minutes, or until the pork is cooked. Remove the pork from the barbecue. Serve immediately with the flavoured butter on top.

NUTRITION PER SERVE
Protein 45.1 g; Fat 32.3 g; Carbohydrate 2.8 g; Dietary Fibre 1.1 g; Cholesterol 268 mg; 2015 kJ (481 Cal)

Add the tomatoes, basil and parmesan to the butter and mix together well.

Spoon the butter into small pots and swirl the surface with a flat-bladed knife.

Trim the pork of excess fat and sinew.

Pepper steaks with horseradish sauce

PREPARATION TIME: 15 MINUTES | TOTAL COOKING TIME: 15 MINUTES | SERVES 4

4 sirloin steaks
3 tablespoons seasoned cracked pepper

HORSERADISH SAUCE
2 tablespoons brandy
3 tablespoons beef stock
4 tablespoons pouring (whipping) cream
1 tablespoon horseradish cream
½ teaspoon sugar

1 Coat the steaks on both sides with pepper, pressing it into the meat. Cook on a hot, lightly oiled barbecue grill plate or flat plate for 5–10 minutes, until cooked to your taste.

2 To make the sauce, put the brandy and stock in a saucepan. Bring to the boil, then reduce the heat. Stir in the cream, horseradish and sugar and heat through. Serve with the steaks.

NUTRITION PER SERVE
Protein 43 g; Fat 21 g; Carbohydrate 2 g; Dietary Fibre 0 g; Cholesterol 130 mg; 1615 kJ (386 Cal)

Press the cracked pepper firmly into both sides of the steaks.

Cook the steaks on a hot, lightly oiled barbecue grill plate or flat plate until they are cooked to your taste.

Add the cream, horseradish and sugar to the brandy and stock in the pan.

Orange and ginger glazed ham

PREPARATION TIME: 25 MINUTES | TOTAL COOKING TIME: 1 HOUR 30 MINUTES | SERVES 20

6 kg (13 lb) cooked ham on the bone
3 tablespoons orange juice
250 g (9 oz/¾ cup) orange marmalade
1 tablespoon grated fresh ginger
2 teaspoons mustard powder
2 tablespoons soft brown sugar
whole cloves (about 30)

1 Prepare a kettle or covered barbecue for indirect cooking at moderate heat (normal fire); see page 249. Run your thumb around the edge of the ham, under the rind, to remove it. Begin pulling from the widest edge. When you've removed the rind to within 10 cm (4 inches) of the shank end, cut through the rind around the shank. Using a sharp knife, remove the excess fat from the ham. (If you like crackling, rub the rind with salt and barbecue for 40 minutes.)

2 Using a sharp knife, score the top of the ham with deep diagonal cuts. Score diagonally the other way, forming a diamond pattern. Place the ham on the barbecue, put the lid on and cook for 45 minutes.

3 Put the juice, marmalade, ginger, mustard and sugar in a small pan. Stir over medium heat until combined, then cool. Remove the ham from the barbecue (so you don't burn yourself). Carefully press the cloves into the top of the ham, one clove per diamond, and brush all over with the marmalade mixture. Return the ham to the barbecue, cover the barbecue and cook for a further 45 minutes. Serve warm or cold.

STORAGE: *Cover the ham with a clean, dry cloth and it will keep in the fridge for up to 1 month. Change the cloth every 2–3 days.*

NUTRITION PER SERVE
Protein 38 g; Fat 7 g; Carbohydrate 8 g; Dietary Fibre 0 g; Cholesterol 102 mg; 1030 kJ (250 Cal)

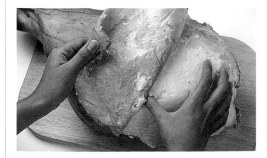

Pull away the ham rind to within 10 cm (4 inches) of the thin shank end.

Score the thin layer of fat on top of the ham with a diagonal pattern.

Lamb chops with citrus pockets

PREPARATION TIME: 25 MINUTES | TOTAL COOKING TIME: 15 MINUTES | SERVES 4

4 lamb chump chops (250 g/9 oz each)
2 tablespoons lemon juice

CITRUS FILLING
3 spring onions (scallions), finely chopped
1 celery stalk, finely chopped
2 teaspoons grated fresh ginger
60 g (2¼ oz/¾ cup) fresh breadcrumbs
2 tablespoons orange juice
2 teaspoons finely grated orange zest
1 teaspoon chopped rosemary

1   Cut a deep, long pocket in the side of each lamb chop.

2   Mix together all the filling ingredients and spoon into the pockets in the lamb.

3   Cook on a hot, lightly oiled barbecue grill plate or flat plate, turning once, for 15 minutes, or until the lamb is almost cooked through but still pink in the centre. Drizzle with the lemon juice.

NUTRITION PER SERVE
Protein 35 g; Fat 5 g; Carbohydrate 15 g; Dietary Fibre 1 g; Cholesterol 105 mg; 1080 kJ (335 Cal)

Cut a deep, long pocket in the side of each lamb chop, right through the skin and fat.

Mix together all the filling ingredients and then spoon into the lamb pockets.

Cook the lamb chops on a hot barbecue grill plate or flat plate, turning once.

Fillet steak with onion marmalade

PREPARATION TIME: 20 MINUTES | TOTAL COOKING TIME: 1 HOUR | SERVES 4

4 thick rib-eye steaks
30 g (1 oz) butter
2 red onions, thinly sliced
2 tablespoons soft brown sugar
1 tablespoon balsamic vinegar

1 Trim any fat from the steaks, then sprinkle liberally with freshly ground black pepper. Cover and refrigerate until ready to cook.

2 To make the onion marmalade, heat the butter in a heavy-based frying pan. Add the onion and cook, stirring often, for 10 minutes over low heat, or until the onion is soft but not brown. Stir in the brown sugar and balsamic vinegar and continue to cook for about 30 minutes, stirring frequently. The mixture will become thick and glossy.

3 Place the steaks on a hot, lightly oiled barbecue grill plate or flat plate and cook for 3 minutes each side to seal, turning once only. For rare steaks, cook a further minute. For medium, cook for another few minutes and for well done, about 5 minutes more. Serve at once with the onion marmalade.

NUTRITION PER SERVE
Protein 30 g; Fat 10 g; Carbohydrate 25 g; Dietary Fibre 4 g; Cholesterol 100 mg; 1355 kJ (320 Cal)

Trim any fat from the steaks and then sprinkle liberally with black pepper.

Cook the onion marmalade for about 40 minutes, or until it is thick and glossy.

Cook the steaks for 3 minutes on each side to seal them, then cook to your taste.

Lamb with eggplant, tomato and pesto

PREPARATION TIME: 30 MINUTES | TOTAL COOKING TIME: 25 MINUTES | SERVES 4

PESTO
100 g (3½ oz/1 bunch) basil
2 garlic cloves, crushed
50 g (1¾ oz/⅓ cup) pine nuts
185 ml (6 fl oz/¾ cup) olive oil
75 g (2½ oz/¾ cup) grated parmesan cheese

1 eggplant (aubergine)
4 roma (plum) tomatoes, halved
6 lamb fillets
60 g (2¼ oz) goat's cheese

1 To make the pesto, finely chop the basil, garlic and pine nuts in a food processor. With the motor running slowly, gradually pour in the olive oil. Add the parmesan and process briefly.

2 Cut the eggplant into thick slices and brush with some olive oil. Cook the eggplant on a hot barbecue grill plate or flat plate, brushing with a little more oil, for 3–4 minutes each side, or until golden brown and softened. Remove and keep warm. Add the tomatoes and cook, brushing with olive oil, until soft. Remove and keep warm.

3 Sprinkle each lamb fillet liberally with black pepper. Wipe the barbecue clean and lightly oil it. Cook the lamb for 3–4 minutes, until cooked through but still pink inside. Slice diagonally and serve with the eggplant, tomato and a little pesto. Crumble the goat's cheese over the top.

NOTE: *Instead of using basil to make the pesto, try coriander (cilantro) or mint, or a mixture of both. For a milder taste, use ricotta or feta rather than goat's cheese.*

NUTRITION PER SERVE
Protein 35 g; Fat 75 g; Carbohydrate 5 g; Dietary Fibre 5 g; Cholesterol 95 mg; 3490 kJ (830 Cal)

Make the pesto in a food processor, finely chopping the basil, garlic and pine nuts first.

Brush the slices of eggplant with olive oil and then grill until golden brown and softened.

The lamb should be cooked through but still pink inside. Slice diagonally to serve.

Veal steaks with caper butter

PREPARATION TIME: 10 MINUTES I TOTAL COOKING TIME: 6 MINUTES I SERVES 4

50 g (1¾ oz) butter, softened
2 tablespoons dry white wine
2 tablespoons capers, finely chopped
2 teaspoons finely grated lemon zest
8 small veal steaks

1 Mix together the butter, white wine, capers, lemon zest and some salt and black pepper with a wooden spoon. Cover and refrigerate until required.

2 Cook the veal steaks on a hot, lightly oiled barbecue grill plate or flat plate for 2–3 minutes on each side. Remove, place on warm plates and top with the caper butter. Serve immediately.

NUTRITION PER SERVE
Protein 30 g; Fat 15 g; Carbohydrate 0 g; Dietary Fibre 0 g; Cholesterol 135 mg; 990 kJ (235 Cal)

Use a sharp knife to finely chop the capers so that they mix smoothly with the butter.

Mix the butter, white wine, capers, lemon zest and salt and pepper.

Cook the veal for 2–3 minutes on each side on a hot barbecue grill plate or flat plate.

Pork loin chops with apple chutney

PREPARATION TIME: 20 MINUTES + AT LEAST 3 HOURS MARINATING | TOTAL COOKING TIME: 25 MINUTES | SERVES 6

6 pork loin chops
4 tablespoons white wine
2 tablespoons oil
2 tablespoons honey
1½ teaspoons ground cumin
2 garlic cloves, crushed

APPLE CHUTNEY
3 green apples
125 ml (4 fl oz/½ cup) apple juice
125 g (4½ oz/½ cup) fruit chutney
15 g (½ oz) butter

1   Trim the chops of excess fat and sinew. Combine the wine, oil, honey, cumin and garlic. Put the chops in a shallow non-metallic dish and then pour in the marinade and toss well to cover. Store, covered with plastic wrap, in the fridge for at least 3 hours, turning occasionally.

2   To make the chutney, peel and dice the apples. Place in a small saucepan with the apple juice. Bring to the boil, reduce the heat and simmer, covered, for 7 minutes or until completely soft. Stir in the chutney and butter and serve warm.

3   Drain the chops, discarding the marinade. Cook the chops on a hot, lightly oiled barbecue grill plate or flat plate for 8 minutes on each side or until tender, turning once. Serve immediately with the chutney.

STORAGE: *The chutney can be kept in the fridge for 1 day before use. It is also delicious with roast pork, lamb chops, chicken cutlets or as a relish with a cheese plate. It can be served warm or cold.*

Simmer until the apple is soft and then stir in the chutney and butter.

Cook the chops on a hot barbecue for 8 minutes on each side.

NUTRITION PER SERVE
Protein 25 g; Fat 10 g; Carbohydrate 29 g; Dietary Fibre 2 g; Cholesterol 55 mg; 1304 kJ (311 Cal)

Leg of lamb with baked vegetables

PREPARATION TIME: 15 MINUTES | TOTAL COOKING TIME: 1 HOUR 30 MINUTES | SERVES 6

LAMB
2 kg (4 lb 8 oz) leg of lamb
4 garlic cloves, cut in half lengthways
6–8 sprigs rosemary
2 tablespoons olive oil

VEGETABLES
6 potatoes
60 g (2¼ oz) butter, melted
¼ teaspoon paprika
750 g (1 lb 10 oz) pumpkin (winter squash)
6 small onions
150 g (5½ oz) green beans, topped and tailed
150 g (5½ oz) broccoli, cut into florets
30 g (1 oz) butter, chopped, extra

1 Prepare a kettle or covered barbecue for indirect cooking at moderate heat (normal fire); see page 249. Place a drip tray on the bottom grill. Trim the meat of excess fat and sinew. Cut narrow, deep slits all over the top and sides of the meat.

2 Push the halved garlic cloves and the rosemary sprigs into the cuts in the meat. Brush all over with oil and sprinkle with 2 tablespoons of freshly ground black pepper.

3 Put the lamb on the barbecue grill over the drip tray, cover and cook for 1 hour 30 minutes for medium-rare meat. Brush with olive oil occasionally. Leave in a warm place, covered with foil, for 10–15 minutes before carving.

4 To prepare the vegetables, peel the potatoes and cut in half. Using a knife, make deep, fine cuts in the potatoes. Do not cut all the way through. Take two sheets of foil, fold in half and brush with melted butter. Place the potatoes on the foil and fold up the edges of the foil to create a tray. Brush the potatoes with melted butter and sprinkle with paprika.

5 Cut the pumpkin into large chunks. Peel the onions and trim the bases, so they will sit flat on the grill. Brush the pumpkin and onions with melted butter. Place the pumpkin, onions and the tray of potatoes on the barbecue grill. Cover the barbecue and cook for 1 hour.

6 Put the beans and broccoli on a sheet of foil brushed with melted butter. Dot with the extra butter and wrap completely in the foil. Add to the other vegetables on the grill and cook for a further 15 minutes.

> NUTRITION PER SERVE
> Protein 49 g; Fat 14 g; Carbohydrate 26 g; Dietary Fibre 6 g; Cholesterol 154 mg; 2105 kJ (500 Cal)

Trim the lamb of excess fat and sinew before making small cuts all over it.

Push the halved cloves of garlic and the rosemary sprigs into the cuts.

Put the pumpkin, onions and tray of potatoes on the barbecue.

Lamb chops with pineapple salsa

PREPARATION TIME: 20 MINUTES | TOTAL COOKING TIME: 10 MINUTES | SERVES 6

12 lamb loin chops
2 tablespoons oil

PINEAPPLE SALSA
½ ripe pineapple (or 400 g/14 oz drained
    tinned pineapple)
1 large red onion, finely chopped
1 fresh red chilli, seeded and diced
1 tablespoon cider or rice vinegar
1 teaspoon sugar
2 tablespoons chopped mint

1 Trim the meat of excess fat and sinew. Brush the chops with oil and season with 1 teaspoon of cracked black pepper.

2 To make the salsa, peel the pineapple, remove the core and eyes and dice the flesh. Toss with the onion, chilli, vinegar, sugar and mint, season with salt and pepper and mix well.

3 Cook the lamb chops on a hot, lightly greased barbecue grill plate or flat plate for 2–3 minutes each side, turning once, until just tender. Serve with the pineapple salsa.

NUTRITION PER SERVE
Protein 33 g; Fat 9 g; Carbohydrate 7 g; Dietary Fibre 2 g; Cholesterol 116 mg; 994 kJ (237 Cal)

Trim the lamb chops of excess fat, brush with oil and season with pepper.

It is a good idea to wear disposable gloves when seeding chillies to prevent skin irritation.

Cook the lamb chops for just 2–3 minutes on each side, turning once.

Sesame and ginger beef

PREPARATION TIME: 15 MINUTES + AT LEAST 2 HOURS MARINATING | TOTAL COOKING TIME: 25 MINUTES | SERVES 4–6

60 ml (2 fl oz/¼ cup) sesame oil

60 ml (2 fl oz/¼ cup) soy sauce

2 garlic cloves, crushed

2 tablespoons grated fresh ginger

1 tablespoon lemon juice

2 tablespoons chopped spring
   onions (scallions)

60 g (2¼ oz/¼ cup) firmly packed soft
   brown sugar

500 g (1 lb 2 oz) piece beef fillet

1 Combine the sesame oil, soy sauce, garlic, ginger, lemon juice, spring onion and brown sugar in a non-metallic dish. Add the beef and coat well with the marinade. Cover and refrigerate for at least 2 hours, or overnight if possible.

2 Drain, reserving the marinade. Brown the beef on all sides on a very hot, lightly oiled barbecue grill plate or flat plate. When the beef is sealed, remove, wrap in foil and return to the barbecue, turning occasionally, for a further 15–20 minutes, depending on how you like your meat. Leave for 10 minutes before slicing.

3 Put the left-over marinade in a pan and boil for 5 minutes. Serve as a sauce with the beef.

NUTRITION PER SERVE (6)
Protein 20 g; Fat 15 g; Carbohydrate 10 g; Dietary Fibre 0 g; Cholesterol 55 mg; 975 kJ (230 Cal)

Combine the sesame oil, soy sauce, garlic, ginger, lemon juice, onion and sugar in a non-metallic dish.

Brown the beef on all sides until the meat is sealed, then remove from the barbecue.

Wrap the beef in foil and then cook on the barbecue, turning occasionally.

Fillet steak with flavoured butters

PREPARATION TIME: 30 MINUTES I TOTAL COOKING TIME: 15 MINUTES I SERVES 4

4 fillet steaks

CAPSICUM BUTTER
1 small red capsicum (pepper)
125 g (4½ oz) butter
2 teaspoons chopped oregano
2 teaspoons snipped chives

GARLIC BUTTER
125 g (4½ oz) butter
3 garlic cloves, crushed
2 spring onions (scallions), finely chopped

1   Cut a pocket in each steak.

2   For the capsicum butter, cut the capsicum into large pieces and place, skin side up, under a hot grill (broiler) until the skin blisters and blackens. Put in a plastic bag until cool. Peel away the skin and finely dice the flesh. Beat the butter until creamy. Add the capsicum and herbs, season and beat until smooth.

3   For the garlic butter, beat the butter until creamy, add the garlic and spring onions and beat until smooth.

4   Push capsicum butter into the pockets in two of the steaks and garlic butter into the other two.

5   Cook on a hot, lightly oiled barbecue grill plate or flat plate for 4–5 minutes each side, turning once. Brush frequently with any remaining flavoured butter while cooking. Serve with barbecued onions.

STORAGE: *The steak can be filled and kept in the fridge for a day. The butters will keep for 2 weeks in the fridge if well covered.*

NUTRITION PER SERVE
Protein 28 g; Fat 57 g; Carbohydrate 2 g; Dietary Fibre 1 g; Cholesterol 244 mg; 2595 kJ (620 Cal)

To make the garlic butter, beat the butter, garlic and spring onions until smooth.

Spoon the flavoured butter into the pocket cut in the side of the steak.

Brush the steaks with any remaining flavoured butter while barbecuing.

Chicken

Chilli chicken with tomato salsa

PREPARATION TIME: 10 MINUTES + AT LEAST 3 HOURS MARINATING | TOTAL COOKING TIME: 20 MINUTES | SERVES 4

8 boneless, skinless chicken thighs
125 ml (4 fl oz/½ cup) lemon juice
¼ teaspoon bottled crushed chilli
2 tablespoons oil
2 teaspoons sesame oil
3 tablespoons soy sauce
3 tablespoons honey
1 garlic clove, crushed
2 spring onions (scallions), chopped
3 tablespoons finely chopped coriander
    (cilantro)

TOMATO SALSA
1 Lebanese (short) cucumber, chopped
1 small red onion, finely chopped
1 tomato, chopped
2 tablespoons olive oil
1 tablespoon white wine vinegar
¼ teaspoon sugar
3 tablespoons chopped coriander (cilantro)

1   Trim the chicken of excess fat and sinew and place in a shallow, non-metallic dish. Mix together the lemon juice, chilli, oils, soy sauce, honey, garlic, spring onion, coriander and salt to taste. Pour over the chicken and toss to coat. Cover and refrigerate for at least 3 hours, stirring occasionally.

2   Drain the chicken, reserving the marinade. Cook on a hot, lightly oiled barbecue grill plate or flat plate for 5–10 minutes on each side, or until tender and cooked through. Brush with reserved marinade occasionally.

3   To make the tomato salsa, mix together the cucumber, onion, tomato, olive oil, vinegar, sugar and coriander in a serving bowl. Serve with the chicken.

STORAGE: *The salsa can be kept, covered, at room temperature for up to a day.*

NUTRITION PER SERVE
Protein 26 g; Fat 22 g; Carbohydrate 15 g; Dietary Fibre 1 g; Cholesterol 55 mg; 1522 kJ (364 Cal)

Mix together the marinade ingredients and marinate the chicken for at least 3 hours.

While the chicken is cooking, baste it occasionally with the marinade.

To make the tomato salsa, simply mix together all the ingredients.

Honey chicken wings

PREPARATION TIME: 10 MINUTES + 2 HOURS MARINATING | TOTAL COOKING TIME: 15 MINUTES | SERVES 4

12 chicken wings
4 tablespoons soy sauce
1 garlic clove, crushed
3 tablespoons sherry
3 tablespoons vegetable oil
3 tablespoons honey

1   Rinse the chicken wings and pat dry with paper towels. Tuck the wing tips to the underside and put in a shallow, non-metallic dish. Combine the soy sauce, garlic, sherry and oil and pour over the chicken. Cover with plastic wrap and refrigerate for 2 hours, turning occasionally.

2   Drain the chicken, discarding the marinade. Cook the chicken on a hot, lightly oiled barbecue grill plate or flat plate for 5 minutes on each side, or until cooked through, turning occasionally. Place the honey in a small heatproof bowl on the edge of the barbecue to warm and thin down a little.

3   Brush the wings with honey and grill for 2 minutes more.

VARIATION: *Try apricot jam instead of the honey for basting. If you prefer a slightly hotter flavour, add some bottled crushed chilli pepper.*

NUTRITION PER SERVE
Protein 46 g; Fat 8 g; Carbohydrate 21 g; Dietary Fibre 2 g; Cholesterol 100 mg; 1411 kJ (337 Cal)

Put the chicken wings in a shallow, non-metallic dish and marinate in the refrigerator.

During the 2 hours of marinating, turn the chicken wings occasionally.

Once the wings are cooked through, brush with the honey and cook for a little longer.

Bacon-wrapped chicken

PREPARATION TIME: 15 MINUTES | TOTAL COOKING TIME: 10 MINUTES | SERVES 6

2 tablespoons olive oil
2 tablespoons lime juice
¼ teaspoon ground coriander
6 boneless, skinless chicken breasts
4 tablespoons fruit chutney
3 tablespoons chopped pecan nuts
6 bacon slices

1 Mix together the oil, lime juice, coriander and salt and pepper to taste. Using a sharp knife, cut a pocket in the thickest section of each chicken breast. Mix together the chutney and nuts. Spoon 1 tablespoon of the chutney mixture into each chicken breast pocket.

2 Turn the tapered ends of the chicken breasts to the underside. Wrap a bacon slice around each breast to enclose the filling and secure with a toothpick.

3 Put the chicken parcels on a hot, lightly oiled barbecue grill plate or flat plate and cook for 5 minutes on each side, or until cooked through, turning once. Brush with the lime juice mixture several times during cooking and drizzle with any left-over lime juice mixture to serve.

VARIATION: *This recipe also works well with prosciutto instead of bacon.*

NUTRITION PER SERVE
Protein 72 g; Fat 28 g; Carbohydrate 19 g; Dietary
Fibre 1 g; Cholesterol 164 mg; 2589 kJ (618 Cal)

Mix together the fruit chutney and pecans to make a filling for the chicken.

Wrap a piece of bacon around each breast and secure with a toothpick or skewer.

Cook the chicken on a hot barbecue grill plate or flat plate for 5 minutes on each side.

Spicy roast chicken with couscous

PREPARATION TIME: 30 MINUTES | TOTAL COOKING TIME: 1 HOUR 15 MINUTES | SERVES 6

1.6 kg (3 lb 8 oz) chicken
90 g (3¼ oz/½ cup) instant couscous
4 pitted dates, chopped
4 dried apricots, chopped
1 tablespoon lime juice
1 tablespoon olive oil
1 tablespoon butter
1 onion, chopped
1–2 garlic cloves, chopped
1 teaspoon ground coriander
2 tablespoons chopped flat-leaf
    (Italian) parsley
1 teaspoon ground cumin
1 tablespoon olive oil, extra

NUTRITION PER SERVE
Protein 46 g; Fat 14 g; Carbohydrate 5.5 g; Dietary
Fibre 1 g; Cholesterol 110 mg; 1378 kJ (329 Cal)

1 Wipe and pat dry the chicken with paper towel. Pour 125 ml (4 fl oz/½ cup) boiling water over the couscous and set aside for 15 minutes for it to swell and soften. Soak the dates and apricots in the lime juice.

2 Heat the oil and butter in a pan, add the onion and garlic and cook for 3–4 minutes, or until translucent. Remove from the heat, add the couscous, soaked dried fruit, coriander and parsley. Mix well and season. Spoon into the chicken cavity and close with a skewer. Tie the legs together with string.

3 Rub the chicken skin all over with a mixture of 1 teaspoon salt, ¼ teaspoon cracked black pepper, cumin and the extra oil. Place in the centre of a large piece of greased foil. Gather the edges together and wrap securely.

4 Place on a barbecue grill over a drip tray. Cover the barbecue and cook for 50 minutes. Open the foil, crimping the edges to form a tray to retain most of the cooking liquid. Cook for a further 20 minutes, or until the chicken is tender and golden. Remove from the heat and leave for 5–6 minutes before carving.

Remove the giblets from the chicken and cut away any large pieces of fat.

Mix the couscous with the other flavourings to make a stuffing.

Rub the chicken skin all over with a mixture of cumin, oil, salt and pepper.

Chicken with salsa verde

PREPARATION TIME: 10 MINUTES I TOTAL COOKING TIME: 10 MINUTES I SERVES 6

SALSA VERDE
1 garlic clove
3 very large handfuls flat-leaf (Italian) parsley
80 ml (2½ fl oz/⅓ cup) extra virgin olive oil
3 tablespoons chopped dill
1½ tablespoons dijon mustard
1 tablespoon sherry vinegar
1 tablespoon baby capers, drained

6 large boneless, skinless chicken breasts

1   Place all the ingredients for the salsa verde in a food processor or blender and process until almost smooth.

2   Cook the chicken on a very hot, lightly oiled barbecue grill plate or flat plate for 4–5 minutes each side, or until cooked through.

3   Cut each chicken breast into three on the diagonal and arrange on serving plates. Top with a spoonful of salsa verde and season to taste.

STORAGE: *The salsa verde can be kept for a day in the fridge.*

NUTRITION PER SERVE
Protein 50 g; Fat 18 g; Carbohydrate 0 g; Dietary Fibre 0.5 g; Cholesterol 110 mg; 1510 kJ (360 Cal)

Put all the salsa verde ingredients in the food processor and process until almost smooth.

Cook the chicken on a very hot barbecue grill plate or flat plate until it is cooked through.

To serve, slice each breast into three on the diagonal and top with salsa verde.

Cajun-spiced drumsticks

PREPARATION TIME: 15 MINUTES + AT LEAST 30 MINUTES STANDING | TOTAL COOKING TIME: 1 HOUR | SERVES 4

1½ tablespoons onion powder
1½ tablespoons garlic powder
2 teaspoons paprika
1 teaspoon white pepper
2 teaspoons dried thyme
½–1 teaspoon chilli powder (see NOTE)
8 chicken drumsticks, scored

1 Combine the herbs, spices and 1 teaspoon salt in a plastic bag. Place the drumsticks in the bag and shake until all the pieces are coated. Leave the chicken in the fridge for at least 30 minutes to allow the flavours to develop, or overnight if time permits.

2 Cook the chicken on a medium hot, lightly oiled barbecue grill for 55–60 minutes, or until slightly blackened and cooked through. Brush lightly with some oil to prevent drying out during cooking.

NOTE: *Chilli powder is very hot, so only use ½ teaspoon if you prefer a milder flavour.*

Put the herbs, spices and salt in a freezer bag, add the chicken and shake to coat.

Cook the chicken for 55–60 minutes, or until slightly blackened.

NUTRITION PER SERVE
Protein 25 g; Fat 7 g; Carbohydrate 0 g; Dietary Fibre 0 g; Cholesterol 103 mg; 660 kJ (160 Cal)

Thai-spiced chicken with potato rosti

PREPARATION TIME: 30 MINUTES + AT LEAST 2 HOURS MARINATING | TOTAL COOKING TIME: 20 MINUTES | SERVES 6

600 g (1 lb 5 oz) chicken tenderloins
    (underbreast fillets)
1 tablespoon chopped fresh lemongrass,
    white part only
2 tablespoons lime juice
1½ tablespoons oil
2 garlic cloves, crushed
1 tablespoon grated fresh ginger
2 teaspoons sweet chilli sauce
2 spring onions (scallions), chopped

POTATO ROSTI
600 g (1 lb 5 oz) potatoes
3 tablespoons plain (all-purpose) flour
1 egg, lightly beaten

1   Remove any excess fat or sinew from the chicken and put it in a shallow, non-metallic dish. Mix together the lemongrass, lime juice, oil, garlic, ginger, sweet chilli sauce and spring onion. Pour over the chicken pieces, cover and refrigerate for at least 2 hours.

2   To make the potato rosti, peel and grate the potatoes. Squeeze the excess moisture from the potato with your hands until it feels quite dry. Mix the potato with the flour and egg and season well. Divide into six equal portions. Cook on a hot, lightly oiled barbecue grill plate or flat plate for 10 minutes, or until golden brown on both sides, flattening them down with the back of a spatula during cooking.

3   Drain the chicken and reserve the marinade. Cook on a barbecue grill plate or flat plate for 3 minutes each side, or until tender and golden brown. Brush with the reserved marinade while cooking. Serve with the rosti.

NUTRITION PER SERVE
Protein 25.9 g; Fat 6.5 g; Carbohydrate 17.6 g; Dietary Fibre 1.9 g; Cholesterol 111 mg; 1003 kJ (239 Cal)

Peel the potatoes and then grate them for making the rosti.

As you cook the rosti, flatten them with the back of a spatula.

Cook the chicken until it is golden brown, brushing with the marinade.

Honey-glazed chicken breasts

PREPARATION TIME: 6 MINUTES + 20 MINUTES MARINATING | TOTAL COOKING TIME: 10 MINUTES | SERVES 6

6 boneless, skinless chicken breasts
50 g (1¾ oz) butter, softened
3 tablespoons honey
3 tablespoons barbecue sauce
2 teaspoons wholegrain mustard

1 Trim the chicken of excess fat and sinew and remove the skin. Use a sharp knife to make three or four diagonal slashes across one side of each chicken breast.

2 Mix together the butter, honey, barbecue sauce and mustard. Spread half of the marinade thickly over the slashed side of the chicken and cover. Set the remaining marinade aside. Leave the chicken at room temperature for 20 minutes.

3 Place the chicken breasts, slashed side up, on a hot, lightly oiled barbecue grill plate or flat plate. Cook for 2–3 minutes each side, or until tender. Brush with the reserved marinade several times during cooking.

STORAGE: *The chicken can be marinated overnight, covered, in the fridge. The longer the chicken is marinated, the more it will take on the marinade flavour, which is quite sweet. If the sweetness is not to your taste, marinate for a shorter time.*

Cut three or four slashes in the chicken breasts so that they cook evenly.

Cook the chicken for 2–3 minutes on each side, brushing with the marinade occasionally.

NUTRITION PER SERVE
Protein 50 g; Fat 18 g; Carbohydrate 0 g; Dietary Fibre 0.5 g; Cholesterol 110 mg; 1510 kJ (360 Cal)

Piri piri chicken

PREPARATION TIME: 5 MINUTES + AT LEAST 1 HOUR MARINATING | TOTAL COOKING TIME: 1 HOUR | SERVES 4

6 bird's eye chillies, with seeds left in,
    finely chopped
1 teaspoon coarse salt
125 ml (4 fl oz/½ cup) olive oil
185 ml (6 fl oz/¾ cup) cider vinegar
1 garlic clove, crushed
4 chicken leg quarters (see NOTE)
lemon wedges, to serve

1   Combine the chilli, salt, olive oil, vinegar and garlic in a screw-top jar. Seal and shake well to combine.

2   Place the chicken pieces in a shallow, non-metallic dish and pour on the marinade. Cover and marinate in the refrigerator for at least 1 hour.

3   Drain the chicken, reserving the marinade. Cook the chicken on a hot, lightly oiled barbecue grill plate or flat plate, basting regularly with the marinade, for 50–60 minutes, or until the chicken is cooked through and the skin begins to crisp. Serve with lemon wedges.

NOTE: *Leg quarters are the drumstick and thigh pieces of the chicken. Any cut of chicken that is still on the bone can be used in this recipe.*

NUTRITION PER SERVE
Protein 27 g; Fat 30 g; Carbohydrate 0.5 g; Dietary Fibre 0.5 g; Cholesterol 60 mg; 1705 kJ (405 Cal)

Put the marinade ingredients in a screw-top jar and shake well to combine.

Pour the marinade over the chicken pieces in the shallow dish.

Cook the chicken on a hot barbecue grill plate or flat plate until the skin begins to crisp.

Buffalo chicken wings with ranch dressing

PREPARATION TIME: 25 MINUTES + 3 HOURS MARINATING | TOTAL COOKING TIME: 10 MINUTES | SERVES 4

8 large chicken wings
2 teaspoons garlic salt
2 teaspoons onion powder
olive oil, for deep-frying
125 ml (4 fl oz/½ cup) tomato sauce
    (ketchup)
2 tablespoons worcestershire sauce
1 tablespoon melted butter
2 teaspoons sugar
Tabasco sauce, to taste

RANCH DRESSING
125 g (4½ oz/½ cup) mayonnaise
125 g (4½ oz/½ cup) sour cream
2 tablespoons lemon juice
2 tablespoons snipped chives

1 Wash the wings thoroughly and pat dry with paper towels. Cut the tip off each wing and discard. Bend each wing back to snap the joint and cut through to create two pieces. Combine 2 teaspoons of black pepper, the garlic salt and onion powder and rub into the wings.

2 Heat the oil to moderately hot in a deep heavy-based pan. Deep-fry the chicken in batches for 2 minutes. Drain on paper towels.

3 Transfer the chicken to a shallow, non-metallic dish. Combine the sauces, butter, sugar and Tabasco and pour over the chicken, stirring to coat. Cover and refrigerate for at least 3 hours.

4 Cook the chicken on a hot, lightly oiled barbecue grill plate or flat plate for 5 minutes, turning and brushing with the marinade.

5 To make the ranch dressing, combine the mayonnaise, cream, juice, chives, salt and pepper and serve with the chicken wings.

NUTRITION PER SERVE
Protein 24 g; Fat 47 g; Carbohydrate 19 g; Dietary
Fibre 1 g; Cholesterol 132 mg; 2478 kJ (592 Cal)

Cut the tips off the wings, then snap them in the middle and cut into two pieces.

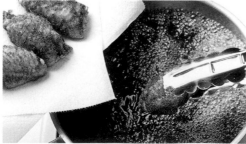
Deep-fry the wings for 2 minutes and then drain on paper towels.

Marinate the chicken in a mixture of butter, sugar, tomato and worcestershire sauces and Tabasco.

Ginger-chilli drumsticks with cucumber yoghurt

PREPARATION TIME: 10 MINUTES + AT LEAST 3 HOURS MARINATING | TOTAL COOKING TIME: 20 MINUTES | SERVES 6

1 tablespoon grated fresh ginger
1 tablespoon brown sugar
1 teaspoon bottled crushed red chilli
¼ teaspoon ground turmeric
1 teaspoon lemon juice
1 teaspoon finely grated lemon zest
250 g (9 oz/1 cup) plain yoghurt
12 chicken drumsticks

CUCUMBER YOGHURT
250 g (9 oz/1 cup) plain yoghurt
½ teaspoon bottled crushed red chilli
1 Lebanese (short) cucumber, peeled, seeded
    and finely chopped
½ teaspoon sugar

1   Mix together the ginger, brown sugar, crushed chilli, turmeric, lemon juice and lemon zest. Stir in the yoghurt. Add the chicken, stirring well to coat. Cover and refrigerate for at least 3 hours, stirring occasionally. Drain, reserving the marinade.

2   Cook the drumsticks on a hot, lightly oiled barbecue grill plate or flat plate for 15–20 minutes, or until tender. Brush occasionally with the reserved marinade.

3   To make the cucumber yoghurt, mix together the yoghurt, crushed chilli, cucumber, sugar and salt to taste and serve with the drumsticks.

Mix together the ginger, sugar, chilli, turmeric, lemon juice and zest and yoghurt.

Cook the drumsticks for 15–20 minutes, brushing occasionally with marinade.

NUTRITION PER SERVE
Protein 45 g; Fat 14 g; Carbohydrate 6 g; Dietary
Fibre 0 g; Cholesterol 190 mg; 1403 kJ (333 Cal)

Chermoula chicken

PREPARATION TIME: 10 MINUTES + AT LEAST 2 HOURS MARINATING | TOTAL COOKING TIME: 15 MINUTES | SERVES 4

1 very large handful flat-leaf (Italian) parsley
1 medium handful coriander (cilantro) leaves
2 garlic cloves, roughly chopped
3 tablespoons lemon juice
1 tablespoon chopped preserved lemon
3 teaspoons ground cumin
125 ml (4 fl oz/½ cup) olive oil
4 boneless, skinless chicken breasts, flattened
    (see NOTE)

1   Mix the parsley, coriander, garlic, lemon juice, preserved lemon and cumin in a food processor until well combined. With the motor running, gradually add the oil in a thin stream until smooth. Season well.

2   Place the chicken in a shallow, non-metallic dish and pour over the marinade. Marinate for at least 2 hours.

3   Grease four sheets of foil and place a chicken breast in the centre of each. Spoon any extra marinade over the chicken. Fold the foil over to seal. Cook the parcels on a hot, lightly oiled barbecue grill plate or flat plate for 10–12 minutes without turning, until cooked through. Remove from the foil and slice.

NOTE: *To flatten chicken breasts, place between two pieces of plastic wrap and hit gently with a meat mallet or rolling pin.*

Put all the ingredients except the chicken in a food processor and mix until smooth.

Once the chicken is cooked, remove from the barbecue onto a tray and open the parcels.

NUTRITION PER SERVE
Protein 25 g; Fat 33 g; Carbohydrate 0.5 g; Dietary Fibre 0.5 g; Cholesterol 60 mg; 1690 kJ (405 Cal)

Spicy chicken with chilli-garlic dip

PREPARATION TIME: 20 MINUTES + 1 HOUR MARINATING I TOTAL COOKING TIME: 25 MINUTES I SERVES 4–6

6 garlic cloves
1 teaspoon black peppercorns
3 coriander (cilantro) roots and stems,
    roughly chopped
12 boneless, skinless chicken thighs
spring onion (scallion), thinly sliced,
    to garnish

CHILLI-GARLIC DIP
4 dried red chillies
2 garlic cloves, chopped
3 tablespoons sugar
4 tablespoons cider or rice vinegar

1   Put the garlic, peppercorns, coriander and ¼ teaspoon of salt in a food processor and process for 20–30 seconds, or until a smooth paste forms, or grind in a mortar and pestle. Trim the chicken of excess fat and sinew. Put it in a shallow, non-metallic dish and spread the paste over the chicken. Cover and leave in the fridge for 1 hour.

2   To make the dip, soak the chillies in hot water for 20 minutes. Drain the chillies and chop finely. Place in a mortar with the garlic and sugar and grind to a smooth paste. Place in a small saucepan, add the vinegar, a pinch of salt and 3 tablespoons boiling water and bring to the boil. Reduce the heat, simmer for 2–3 minutes and cool.

3   Cook the chicken on a hot, lightly oiled barbecue grill plate or flat plate for 5–10 minutes each side, turning once. Serve with the dip and garnish with spring onion.

STORAGE: *The chicken can be kept in the marinade in the fridge for up to a day. The dip can be made 3 days in advance.*

NUTRITION PER SERVE (6)
Protein 47 g; Fat 5 g; Carbohydrate 0.5 g; Dietary Fibre 1 g; Cholesterol 105 mg; 1005 kJ (240 Cal)

Trim the chicken of excess fat and sinew before spreading the paste over it.

Mix together the garlic, peppercorns, coriander and salt in a food processor.

Grind the chillies, garlic and sugar to a smooth paste with a mortar and pestle.

Tandoori chicken

PREPARATION TIME: 10 MINUTES + AT LEAST 1 HOUR MARINATING | TOTAL COOKING TIME: 10 MINUTES | SERVES 4

125 g (4½ oz/½ cup) Greek-style yoghurt
2 tablespoons tandoori paste
2 garlic cloves, crushed
2 tablespoons lime juice
1½ teaspoons garam masala
2 tablespoons finely chopped coriander
   (cilantro) leaves
6 boneless, skinless chicken thighs
cucumber raita and naan bread, to serve

1 Combine the yoghurt, tandoori paste, garlic, lime juice, garam masala and coriander in a bowl and mix well.

2 Add the chicken, coat well, cover and refrigerate for at least 1 hour.

3 Cook the chicken on a hot, lightly oiled barbecue grill plate or flat plate for 5 minutes on each side, basting with the remaining marinade, until golden and cooked through. Serve with cucumber raita and naan bread.

NUTRITION PER SERVE
Protein 27 g; Fat 3.5 g; Carbohydrate 2 g; Dietary Fibre 0 g; Cholesterol 60 mg; 635 kJ (150 Cal)

Mix together the yoghurt, tandoori paste, garlic, lime juice, garam masala and coriander.

Add the chicken to the marinade and leave for at least an hour.

Cook the chicken on a barbecue grill plate or flat plate for 5 minutes on each side.

Chicken breasts with lime and ginger glaze

PREPARATION TIME: 10 MINUTES + AT LEAST 2 HOURS MARINATING | TOTAL COOKING TIME: 15–20 MINUTES | SERVES 6

6 boneless, skinless chicken breasts

LIME AND GINGER GLAZE
160 g (5¾ oz/½ cup) lime marmalade
60 ml (2 fl oz/¼ cup) lime juice
2 tablespoons sherry
2 tablespoons soft brown sugar
2 teaspoons finely grated fresh ginger
grilled lime halves, to serve

1 Trim the chicken of excess fat and sinew. Use a sharp knife to make three or four diagonal slashes across one side of each chicken breast. Place chicken in a non-metallic dish.

2 Put the lime marmalade, lime juice, sherry, soft brown sugar and fresh ginger in a saucepan. Stir over low heat until melted together.

3 Pour over the chicken and toss well to combine. Cover and refrigerate for at least 2 hours or overnight (overnight is best, time permitting).

4 Drain the chicken, discarding the marinade. Place the chicken breasts, slashed side up, on a hot, lightly oiled barbecue grill plate or flat plate. Cook for 10 minutes, or until cooked through. Serve with grilled lime halves.

Cut three or four slashes in the chicken breasts so that they cook evenly.

Stir the lime and ginger glaze ingredients over low heat until melted, then pour over the chicken.

NUTRITION PER SERVE
Protein 39.7 g; Fat 3.3 g; Carbohydrate 22 g; Dietary Fibre 0.3 g; Cholesterol 117 mg; 1189 kJ (284 Cal)

Garlic roast chicken

PREPARATION TIME: 10 MINUTES | TOTAL COOKING TIME: 1 HOUR | SERVES 6

1.8 kg (4 lb) chicken
1 bulb garlic
small bunch oregano
3 tablespoons olive oil

1 Prepare a kettle or covered barbecue for indirect cooking at moderate heat (normal fire); see page 249. Place a drip tray under the top grill. Wipe the chicken and pat dry with paper towel. Season the cavity with salt and ½ teaspoon cracked peppercorns. Using a sharp knife, cut the top off the bulb of garlic. Push the whole bulb of garlic, unpeeled, into the cavity. Follow with the whole bunch of oregano. Close the cavity with several toothpicks or a skewer.

2 Rub the chicken skin with salt and brush with oil. Place on the barbecue over the drip tray. Cover and cook for 1 hour, brushing occasionally with olive oil to keep the skin moist. Test the chicken by poking a skewer into the thigh—if the juices run clear, the chicken is cooked through. Leave the chicken for 5 minutes before carving.

3 Carefully separate the garlic cloves and serve 1 or 2 cloves with each serving of chicken. (The soft flesh can be squeezed from the clove and eaten with the chicken.)

STORAGE: *The chicken can be kept warm in the barbecue with the top and bottom vents open.*

HINT: *Toast slices of French bread and spread with the soft, cooked garlic. Add a drizzle of olive oil and season with salt and pepper.*

NUTRITION PER SERVE
Protein 21 g; Fat 14 g; Carbohydrate 0 g; Dietary Fibre 0 g; Cholesterol 70 mg; 875 kJ (210 Cal)

Cut the top off the bulb of garlic and then cook in the cavity of the chicken.

Test that the chicken is cooked by poking the thickest part of the thigh with a skewer.

Separate the cooked cloves of garlic and serve a couple with each portion of chicken.

Hoisin barbecued chicken

PREPARATION TIME: 10 MINUTES + AT LEAST 2 HOURS MARINATING | TOTAL COOKING TIME: 25 MINUTES | SERVES 6

2 garlic cloves, finely chopped
60 ml (2 fl oz/¼ cup) hoisin sauce
3 teaspoons light soy sauce
3 teaspoons honey
2 tablespoons tomato sauce (ketchup) or sweet chilli sauce
1 teaspoon sesame oil
2 spring onions (scallions), finely sliced
1.5 kg (3 lb 5 oz) chicken wings

1 To make the marinade, mix together the garlic, hoisin sauce, soy sauce, honey, tomato sauce, sesame oil and spring onion.

2 Put the chicken wings in a shallow, non-metallic dish, add the marinade, cover and leave in the fridge for at least 2 hours.

3 Drain the chicken, reserving the marinade. Cook the chicken on a hot, lightly oiled barbecue grill plate or flat plate, turning once, for 20–25 minutes, or until cooked through and golden brown. Baste with the marinade during cooking. Heat any remaining marinade in a pan until boiling, boil for 3 minutes and serve as a sauce.

NUTRITION PER SERVE
Protein 26 g; Fat 8.5 g; Carbohydrate 9 g; Dietary Fibre 1.5 g; Cholesterol 111 mg; 916 kJ (219 Cal)

Mix together the garlic, hoisin sauce, soy sauce, honey, tomato sauce, sesame oil and spring onions.

Pour the marinade over the chicken, cover the dish and leave in the fridge.

Cook the chicken for 20–25 minutes, or until cooked and golden brown.

Teriyaki chicken wings

PREPARATION TIME: 15 MINUTES + AT LEAST 3 HOURS MARINATING | TOTAL COOKING TIME: 15 MINUTES | SERVES 4

8 chicken wings
3 tablespoons soy sauce
2 tablespoons sherry
2 teaspoons grated fresh ginger
1 garlic clove, crushed
1 tablespoon honey

1 Wash the chicken wings and pat dry with paper towels. Trim any excess fat from the wings and tuck the tips under to form a triangle. Place in a shallow non-metallic dish.

2 Mix together the soy sauce, sherry, ginger, garlic and honey. Pour over the chicken, cover and leave to marinate in the fridge for at least 3 hours. Drain the chicken, reserving the marinade. Lightly brush two sheets of foil with oil. Place 4 wings in a single layer on each piece of foil and wrap completely in a parcel.

3 Cook the parcels on a hot barbecue grill plate or flat plate for 10 minutes. Unwrap, then place the wings directly on a lightly greased grill and cook for 3 minutes, or until brown. Turn them frequently and brush with any remaining marinade.

STORAGE: *The chicken can be left in the marinade in the fridge for up to 2 days.*

NUTRITION PER SERVE
Protein 16 g; Fat 7 g; Carbohydrate 6 g; Dietary Fibre 0 g; Cholesterol 46 mg; 700 kJ (167 Cal)

Trim the excess fat from the wings and tuck the tips under to make triangles.

Place four wings in a single layer on each sheet of foil and make a parcel.

Unwrap the wings from the parcels and place directly on the barbecue grill plate or flat plate.

Chicken cutlets with corn relish

PREPARATION TIME: 20 MINUTES | TOTAL COOKING TIME: 30 MINUTES | SERVES 4

8 boneless chicken thigh cutlets with skin
1 tablespoon olive oil
1 garlic clove, crushed
¼ teaspoon ground turmeric

CORN RELISH
200 g (7 oz/1 cup) corn kernels,
    fresh or tinned
1 tablespoon olive oil
1 red chilli, seeded and chopped
1 small green capsicum (pepper),
    finely chopped
1 onion, finely chopped
4 tablespoons white vinegar
3 tablespoons sugar
1 teaspoon wholegrain mustard
3 teaspoons cornflour (cornstarch)
1 teaspoon paprika
1 teaspoon finely chopped coriander
    (cilantro) leaves
1 tablespoon olive oil, extra

1   Prick the chicken skin and put in a large frying pan of boiling water. Simmer for 5 minutes. Drain and cool. Mix the olive oil, garlic, turmeric and ½ teaspoon salt and rub over the skin of the chicken.

2   To make the relish, cook the fresh corn in boiling water for 2–3 minutes or until tender, then drain. (If using tinned corn, drain, but do not cook.) Heat the oil in a pan. Add the chilli, capsicum and onion and cook until tender. Add the corn, vinegar, sugar and mustard and cook, stirring, for a further 5 minutes. Blend the cornflour with 125 ml (4 fl oz/½ cup) water until smooth and add to the relish. Bring to the boil, reduce the heat and stir until thickened. Stir in the paprika, coriander and extra oil. Leave to cool.

3   Cook the chicken, skin side up, on a hot, lightly oiled barbecue grill plate or flat plate for 2 minutes, then turn and cook for 4 minutes. Continue cooking for another 5–10 minutes, turning frequently, until the chicken is well browned and cooked through. Serve with the corn relish.

STORAGE: *The corn relish will keep for up to 4 days in a jar in the fridge.*

NUTRITION PER SERVE
Protein 36 g; Fat 39 g; Carbohydrate 14 g; Dietary Fibre 1 g; Cholesterol 110 mg; 2280 kJ (545 Cal)

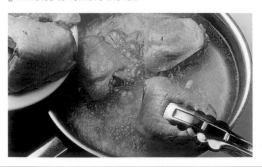
Prick the chicken skin and simmer in water for 5 minutes to remove the fat.

Mix the cornflour with water until smooth and then add to the relish.

Cook the cutlets, skin side up for 2 minutes, then turn frequently during the remaining cooking time.

Barbecued garlic chicken

PREPARATION TIME: 20 MINUTES + AT LEAST 2 HOURS MARINATING | TOTAL COOKING TIME: 10 MINUTES | SERVES 4

6 garlic cloves, crushed
1½ tablespoons cracked black peppercorns
3 large handfuls coriander (cilantro) leaves
    and stems, chopped
4 coriander (cilantro) roots, chopped
80 ml (2½ fl oz/⅓ cup) lime juice
1 teaspoon soft brown sugar
1 teaspoon ground turmeric
2 teaspoons light soy sauce
4 boneless, skinless chicken breasts

CUCUMBER AND TOMATO SALAD
1 Lebanese (short) cucumber
1 large roma (plum) tomato
¼ small red onion, thinly sliced
1 small red or green chilli, diced
2 tablespoons coriander (cilantro) leaves
2 tablespoons lime juice
1 teaspoon soft brown sugar
1 tablespoon fish sauce

1 Blend the garlic, peppercorns, coriander, lime juice, sugar, turmeric and soy sauce until smooth in a food processor or mortar and pestle.

2 Separate the tenderloins (underbreast fillets) from the breasts. Put the chicken in a shallow, non-metallic dish, add the marinade, cover and refrigerate for 2 hours or overnight, turning occasionally.

3 To make the salad, halve the cucumber lengthways and scoop out the seeds with a teaspoon. Cut into slices. Halve the tomato lengthways and slice. Combine the cucumber, tomato, onion, chilli and coriander. Drizzle with the combined lime juice, sugar and fish sauce.

4 Cook the chicken on a hot, lightly oiled barbecue grill plate or flat plate for 4 minutes on each side, or until tender. The tenderloins will take less time to cook. Serve with the salad.

NUTRITION PER SERVE
Protein 41.6 g; Fat 3.1 g; Carbohydrate 6 g; Dietary Fibre 1.5 g; Cholesterol 117 mg; 960 kJ (229 Cal)

Add the chopped coriander roots to the other ingredients and blend until smooth.

The tenderloins are the small fillets underneath the breasts. Separate them because they cook quicker.

Use a teaspoon to scoop the seeds out of the halved cucumber.

Crispy chicken wings

PREPARATION TIME: 10 MINUTES + AT LEAST 2 HOURS MARINATING | TOTAL COOKING TIME: 15 MINUTES | SERVES 6

12 chicken wings
3 tablespoons soy sauce
3 tablespoons hoisin sauce
125 g (4½ oz/½ cup) tomato sauce (ketchup)
2 tablespoons honey
1 tablespoon brown sugar
1 tablespoon cider vinegar
2 garlic cloves, crushed
¼ teaspoon Chinese five-spice powder
2 teaspoons sesame oil

1 Tuck the chicken wing tips to the underside and place in a non-metallic bowl.

2 Mix together all the remaining ingredients and pour over the wings, tossing to coat. Cover and leave in the fridge for at least 2 hours, turning occasionally. Drain, reserving the marinade.

3 Cook the wings on a hot, lightly oiled barbecue grill plate or flat plate for 15 minutes, or until cooked through, brushing with the reserved marinade several times.

NUTRITION PER SERVE
Protein 46 g; Fat 8 g; Carbohydrate 21 g; Dietary Fibre 2 g; Cholesterol 100 mg; 1411 kJ (337 Cal)

Tuck the chicken wing tips to the underside so the wings form triangle shapes.

Mix together all the remaining ingredients to make a marinade for the chicken.

Place the chicken on a hot, lightly oiled barbecue grill plate or flat plate and cook for 15 minutes.

Citrus chicken drumsticks

PREPARATION TIME: 20 MINUTES + AT LEAST 3 HOURS MARINATING | TOTAL COOKING TIME: 20 MINUTES | SERVES 4

8 chicken drumsticks
4 tablespoons orange juice
4 tablespoons lemon juice
1 teaspoon grated orange zest
1 teaspoon grated lemon zest
1 teaspoon sesame oil
1 tablespoon olive oil
1 spring onion (scallion), finely chopped

1 Score the thickest part of the chicken so that it cooks evenly. Place in a shallow non-metallic dish.

2 Combine the juices, zests, oils and spring onion and pour over the chicken. Cover and leave in the fridge for at least 3 hours, turning occasionally. Drain the chicken, reserving the marinade.

3 Cook the drumsticks on a hot, lightly oiled barbecue grill plate or flat plate for 15–20 minutes, or until tender. Brush occasionally with the reserved marinade. Serve immediately.

NUTRITION PER SERVE
Protein 24 g; Fat 13 g; Carbohydrate 3 g; Dietary Fibre 0 g; Cholesterol 103 mg; 949 kJ (227 Cal)

Score the thickest part of the chicken with a knife so that it cooks evenly.

Put the chicken in a non-metallic dish so that the citrus in the marinade doesn't react with the metal.

While the chicken is cooking, brush it occasionally with the marinade.

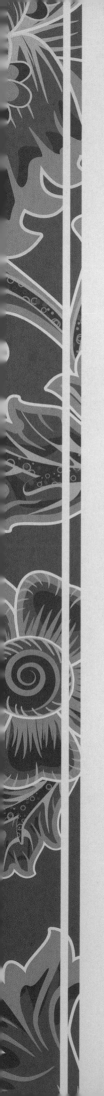

Seafood

Barbecued shellfish platter

PREPARATION TIME: 40 MINUTES + 1 HOUR FREEZING | TOTAL COOKING TIME: 30 MINUTES | SERVES 6

6 live moreton bay bugs (flat-head lobsters)
30 g (1 oz) butter, melted
1 tablespoon oil
12 black mussels
12 scallops on their shells
12 oysters on their shells
18 raw large prawns (shrimp), unpeeled

SALSA VERDE, FOR SCALLOPS
1 tablespoon finely chopped preserved lemon
2 large handfuls parsley
1 tablespoon drained bottled capers
1 tablespoon lemon juice
3 tablespoons oil, approximately

VINEGAR AND SHALLOT
DRESSING, FOR MUSSELS
60 ml (2 fl oz/¼ cup) white wine vinegar
4 French shallots (eschalots), finely chopped
1 tablespoon chopped chervil

PICKLED GINGER AND WASABI
SAUCE, FOR OYSTERS
1 teaspoon soy sauce
60 ml (2 fl oz/¼ cup) mirin
2 tablespoons rice wine vinegar
¼ teaspoon wasabi paste
2 tablespoons finely sliced pickled ginger

SWEET BALSAMIC DRESSING,
FOR MORETON BAY BUGS
1 tablespoon olive oil
1 tablespoon honey
125 ml (4 fl oz/½ cup) balsamic vinegar

THAI CORIANDER SAUCE,
FOR PRAWNS
125 ml (4 fl oz/½ cup) sweet chilli sauce
1 tablespoon lime juice
2 tablespoons chopped coriander (cilantro)

NUTRITION PER SERVE
Protein 42.1 g; Fat 22.5 g; Carbohydrate 21.4 g; Dietary
Fibre 0.6 g; Cholesterol 242 mg; 1952 kJ (466 Cal)

1   Freeze the bugs for 1 hour to immobilise.
Cut each bug in half by turning each one
upside down, inserting a knife through the shell
between the legs and cutting through. Repeat,
cutting through the tail. Brush the flesh with
the combined butter and oil. Set aside while
you prepare the rest of the seafood.

2   Scrub the mussels with a stiff brush and
pull off the hairy beards. Discard any broken
mussels, or open ones that don't close when
tapped on a work surface. Rinse well.

3   Slice or pull off any vein, membrane or hard
white muscle from the scallops, leaving any roe
attached. Brush the scallops with butter.

4   Remove the oysters from the shells, then
rinse the shells under cold water. Pat dry and
return the oysters to their shells. Cover and
refrigerate all the seafood while you make
the dressings.

5   For the salsa verde, combine all the
ingredients except the oil in a food processor
and process in short bursts until roughly
chopped. Transfer to a bowl and add enough
oil to moisten. Season with salt and pepper.

6   For the vinegar and shallot dressing,
whisk the vinegar, shallots and chervil in
a bowl until combined.

7   For the pickled ginger and wasabi
sauce, whisk all the ingredients in a bowl
until combined.

8   For the sweet balsamic dressing, heat the
oil in a saucepan, add the honey and vinegar
and bring to the boil, then boil until reduced
by half.

9   For the Thai coriander sauce, combine all
the ingredients in a bowl.

10 Cook the seafood on a hot, lightly oiled
hotplate. The moreton bay bug will take the
longest time to cook, about 5 minutes. The
mussels, scallops, oysters and prawns all take
about 2–5 minutes to cook. Serve the seafood
with their dressings.

Coriander prawns

PREPARATION TIME: 15 MINUTES + 30 MINUTES MARINATING | TOTAL COOKING TIME: 5 MINUTES | SERVES 4

8 very large raw prawns (shrimp)
1 tablespoon sweet chilli sauce
1 teaspoon ground coriander
125 ml (4 fl oz/½ cup) olive oil
80 ml (2½ fl oz/⅓ cup) lime juice
3 garlic cloves, crushed
1 tomato, peeled, seeded and chopped
2 tablespoons roughly chopped coriander
   (cilantro)

1 Remove the heads from the prawns and, with a sharp knife, cut the prawns in half lengthways, leaving the tails attached. Pull out each dark vein along the back of the prawn.

2 Mix together the sweet chilli sauce and ground coriander with half the olive oil, half the lime juice and half the garlic. Add the prawns, toss to coat, then cover and marinate in the fridge for 30 minutes.

3 Meanwhile, to make the dressing, mix the remaining olive oil, lime juice and garlic in a bowl with the chopped tomato and coriander.

4 Drain the prawns, reserving the marinade, and cook, cut side down, on a hot, lightly oiled barbecue grill plate or flat plate for 1–2 minutes each side, or until cooked through, brushing occasionally with the marinade.

5 Spoon a little of the dressing over the prawns and season well before serving.

Cut each prawn through the centre lengthways, leaving the tail attached.

Cook both sides of the drained prawns on a hot barbecue grill plate or flat plate.

NUTRITION PER SERVE
Protein 42 g; Fat 31 g; Carbohydrate 2.5 g; Dietary Fibre 2 g; Cholesterol 298 mg; 1930 kJ (460 Cal)

Balsamic baby octopus

PREPARATION TIME: 15 MINUTES + AT LEAST 3 HOURS MARINATING I TOTAL COOKING TIME: 10 MINUTES I SERVES 4

1 kg (2 lb 4 oz) baby octopus
185 ml (6 fl oz/¾ cup) red wine
2 tablespoons balsamic vinegar
2 tablespoons soy sauce
2 tablespoons hoisin sauce
1 garlic clove, crushed

1 Cut off the octopus heads, below the eyes, with a sharp knife. Discard the heads and guts. Push the beaks out with your index finger, remove and discard. Wash the octopus thoroughly under running water and drain on crumpled paper towels. If the octopus tentacles are large, cut into quarters.

2 Put the octopus in a large bowl. Stir together the wine, vinegar, soy sauce, hoisin sauce and garlic and pour over the octopus. Toss to coat, then cover and refrigerate for at least 3 hours. Drain the octopus, reserving the left-over marinade.

3 Cook on a very hot, lightly oiled barbecue grill plate or flat plate, in batches, for 3–5 minutes, or until the octopus flesh turns white. Brush the marinade over the octopus during cooking. Be careful not to overcook or the octopus will be tough. Serve warm or cold.

NUTRITION PER SERVE
Protein 42.5 g; Fat 3.5 g; Carbohydrate 4 g; Dietary Fibre 1 g; Cholesterol 497.5 mg; 1060 kJ (255 Cal)

Remove and discard the head from each octopus using a sharp knife.

Push the hard, dark beak through the centre with your index finger.

Brush the octopus all over with the reserved marinade while cooking.

Tuna with caponata

PREPARATION TIME: 25 MINUTES + 1 HOUR STANDING | TOTAL COOKING TIME: 50 MINUTES | SERVES 6

CAPONATA
750 g (1 lb 10 oz) eggplant (aubergine), diced
80 ml (2½ fl oz/⅓ cup) olive oil
500 g (1 lb 2 oz) ripe tomatoes
2 tablespoons olive oil, extra
1 onion, chopped
3 celery stalks, chopped
2 tablespoons drained capers
90 g (3¼ oz/½ cup) green olives, pitted
1 tablespoon sugar
125 ml (4 fl oz/½ cup) red wine vinegar

6 x 200 g (7 oz) tuna steaks

NUTRITION PER SERVE
Protein 45 g; Fat 30 g; Carbohydrate 7 g; Dietary
Fibre 5 g; Cholesterol 140 mg; 1963 kJ (470 Cal)

1   Place the eggplant in a colander, sprinkle with salt and leave for 1 hour. Rinse under cold running water and pat dry. Heat the oil in a frying pan and cook the eggplant, in batches, for 4–5 minutes, or until golden and soft. Remove from the pan.

2   To prepare the tomatoes, score a cross in the base of each tomato. Place in a bowl of boiling water for 1 minute, then plunge into cold water and peel the skin away from the cross. Cut into small cubes.

3   Heat the extra oil in the pan, add the onion and celery and cook for 3–4 minutes, or until golden. Reduce the heat to low, add the tomato and simmer for 15 minutes, stirring occasionally. Stir in the capers, olives, sugar and vinegar, season and simmer, stirring occasionally, for 10 minutes, or until slightly reduced. Stir in the eggplant. Allow to cool.

4   Cook the tuna on a hot, lightly oiled barbecue grill plate or flat plate for 2–3 minutes each side, or until cooked to your liking. Serve immediately with the caponata.

Cook the eggplant (in batches if your frying pan is small), until golden and soft.

Add the capers, olives, sugar and vinegar to the tomato mixture.

Cook the tuna on a hot barbecue until cooked to your taste.

Barbecued sardines

PREPARATION TIME: 25 MINUTES + 2 HOURS MARINATING I TOTAL COOKING TIME: 10 MINUTES I SERVES 4

8 large fresh sardines
8 sprigs lemon thyme
3 tablespoons extra virgin olive oil
2 garlic cloves, crushed
1 teaspoon finely grated lemon zest
2 tablespoons lemon juice
1 teaspoon ground cumin
lemon wedges, for serving

1   Carefully slit the sardines from head to tail and remove the gut. Rinse, then pat dry inside and out with paper towels. Place a sprig of lemon thyme in each fish cavity and arrange the fish in a shallow non-metallic dish.

2   Combine the olive oil, garlic, lemon zest, lemon juice and cumin and pour over the fish. Cover and refrigerate for 2 hours.

3   Cook on a hot, lightly oiled barbecue grill plate or flat plate for 2–3 minutes each side, basting frequently with the marinade, or until the flesh flakes easily when tested with a fork. Alternatively, barbecue in a sardine cooking rack until tender. Serve with lemon wedges.

NUTRITION PER SERVE
Protein 46 g; Fat 12 g; Carbohydrate 0 g; Dietary
Fibre 1 g; Cholesterol 180 mg; 1200 kJ (245 Cal)

Slit the sardine from head to tail with a sharp knife and then remove the gut.

Place a sprig of lemon thyme in the cavity of each fish and put in a shallow dish to marinate.

Cook the sardines until the flesh flakes easily when tested with a fork.

Squid with picada dressing

PREPARATION TIME: 40 MINUTES + 30 MINUTES REFRIGERATION | TOTAL COOKING TIME: 10 MINUTES | SERVES 6

500 g (1 lb 2 oz) small squid (see NOTE)

PICADA DRESSING
2 tablespoons extra virgin olive oil
2 tablespoons finely chopped flat-leaf (Italian)
    parsley
1 garlic clove, crushed

1   To clean the squid, gently pull the tentacles away from the tube (the intestines should come away at the same time). Remove the intestines from the tentacles by cutting under the eyes, then remove the beak, if it remains in the centre of the tentacles, by pushing up with your index finger. Pull away the quill (the transparent membrane) and discard.

2   Rub the tubes under cold running water and the skin should come away easily. Wash the tubes and tentacles and drain well. Place in a bowl, add ¼ teaspoon of salt and mix well. Cover and refrigerate for about 30 minutes.

3   For the picada dressing, whisk together the olive oil, parsley, garlic, ¼ teaspoon of cracked black pepper and some salt.

4   Cook the squid tubes in small batches on a very hot, lightly oiled barbecue grill plate or flat plate for 2–3 minutes, or until white and tender. Barbecue or grill the squid tentacles, turning to brown them all over, for 1 minute, or until they curl up. Serve hot, drizzled with the picada dressing.

NOTE: *A suitably small variety of squid is the bottleneck squid.*

STORAGE: *Make the picada dressing as close to serving time as possible so the parsley doesn't discolour.*

NUTRITION PER SERVE
Protein 20 g; Fat 10 g; Carbohydrate 1 g; Dietary Fibre 1 g; Cholesterol 180 mg; 800 kJ (190 Cal)

Gently pull the tentacles away from the squid tubes and the intestines should follow.

Cut under the eyes to remove the intestines and then remove the beak.

Barbecued tuna and white bean salad

PREPARATION TIME: 25 MINUTES I TOTAL COOKING TIME: 5 MINUTES I SERVES 4–6

400 g (14 oz) tuna steaks
1 small red onion, thinly sliced
1 tomato, seeded and chopped
1 small red capsicum (pepper), thinly sliced
2 x 400 g (14 oz) tins cannellini beans
2 garlic cloves, crushed
1 teaspoon chopped thyme
4 tablespoons finely chopped flat-leaf
    (Italian) parsley
1½ tablespoons lemon juice
80 ml (2½ fl oz/⅓ cup) extra virgin olive oil
1 teaspoon honey
100 g (3½ oz) rocket leaves

NUTRITION PER SERVE (6)
Protein 30 g; Fat 20 g; Carbohydrate 17 g; Dietary
Fibre 10 g; Cholesterol 0 mg; 1656 kJ (394 Cal)

1   Place the tuna steaks on a plate, sprinkle with cracked black pepper on both sides, cover with plastic and refrigerate until needed.

2   Combine the onion, tomato and capsicum in a large bowl. Rinse the cannellini beans under cold running water for 30 seconds, drain and add to the bowl with the garlic, thyme and 3 tablespoons of the parsley.

3   Place the lemon juice, oil and honey in a small saucepan, bring to the boil, then simmer, stirring, for 1 minute, or until the honey melts. Remove from the heat.

4   Cook the tuna on a hot, lightly oiled barbecue grill plate or flat plate for 1 minute on each side. The meat should still be pink in the middle. Slice into small cubes and combine with the salad. Toss with the warm dressing.

5   Arrange the rocket on a platter. Top with the salad, season well and toss with the remaining parsley.

Add the beans, garlic, thyme and parsley to the bowl and mix well.

Heat the lemon juice, oil and honey in a saucepan until the honey melts.

Cook the tuna until still pink in the middle, then cut into small cubes.

Thai-style whole snapper

PREPARATION TIME: 10 MINUTES | TOTAL COOKING TIME: 30 MINUTES | SERVES 4–6

2 garlic cloves, crushed
1 tablespoon fish sauce
2 tablespoons lemon juice
1 tablespoon grated fresh ginger
2 tablespoons sweet chilli sauce
2 tablespoons chopped coriander (cilantro)
1 tablespoon rice wine vinegar
2 tablespoons white wine
600 g (1 lb 5 oz) whole snapper, cleaned
    and scaled
2 spring onions (scallions), cut into
    very fine shreds

1   Mix together the garlic, fish sauce, lemon juice, ginger, chilli sauce, coriander, rice wine vinegar and wine.

2   Place the snapper on a large piece of double-thickness foil. Pour the marinade over the fish and sprinkle with the spring onion.

3   Wrap the fish in the foil to make a parcel. Cook over medium heat on a barbecue grill plate or flat plate for 20–30 minutes, or until the flesh flakes easily when tested with a fork.

NUTRITION PER SERVE (6)
Protein 20 g; Fat 2 g; Carbohydrate 5 g; Dietary
Fibre 0 g; Cholesterol 60 mg; 495 kJ (120 Cal)

Mix together the garlic, fish sauce, lemon juice, ginger, chilli sauce, coriander, vinegar and wine.

Pour the marinade over the snapper after you have placed it on the foil.

Cook the fish until the flesh flakes easily when tested with a fork.

King prawns with dill mayonnaise

PREPARATION TIME: 40 MINUTES + AT LEAST 2 HOURS MARINATING | TOTAL COOKING TIME: 10–15 MINUTES | SERVES 4

MARINADE
125 ml (4 fl oz/½ cup) olive oil
80 ml (2½ fl oz/⅓ cup) lemon juice
2 tablespoons wholegrain mustard
2 tablespoons honey
2 tablespoons chopped dill

16 raw king prawns (shrimp)

DILL MAYONNAISE
185 g (6½ oz/¾ cup) mayonnaise
2 tablespoons chopped dill
1½ tablespoons lemon juice
1 gherkin (pickle), finely chopped
1 teaspoon chopped capers
1 garlic clove, crushed

1 To make the marinade, combine the olive oil, lemon juice, mustard, honey and dill, pour over the unpeeled prawns and coat well. Cover and refrigerate for at least 2 hours, turning occasionally.

2 To make the dill mayonnaise, whisk together the mayonnaise, dill, lemon juice, gherkin, capers and garlic. Cover and refrigerate.

3 Cook the drained prawns on a hot, lightly oiled barbecue grill plate or flat plate in batches for 4 minutes, turning frequently, until pink and cooked through. Serve with the mayonnaise.

NUTRITION PER SERVE
Protein 20 g; Fat 45 g; Carbohydrate 25 g; Dietary Fibre 1 g; Cholesterol 155 mg; 405 kJ (570 Cal)

Mix together the marinade ingredients and pour over the unpeeled prawns.

Whisk together the mayonnaise, dill, lemon juice, gherkin, capers and garlic.

Lemon and herb trout

PREPARATION TIME: 20 MINUTES | TOTAL COOKING TIME: 15 MINUTES | SERVES 4

3 tablespoons chopped dill
2 tablespoons chopped rosemary
3 tablespoons coarsely chopped flat-leaf
  (Italian) parsley
2 teaspoons thyme
6 teaspoons crushed green peppercorns
80 ml (2½ fl oz/⅓ cup) lemon juice
1 lemon
4 whole fresh trout
80 ml (2½ fl oz/⅓ cup) dry white wine

HORSERADISH CREAM
1 tablespoon horseradish cream
125 g (4½ oz/½ cup) sour cream
2 tablespoons pouring (whipping) cream

LEMON SAUCE
2 egg yolks
150 g (5½ oz) butter, melted
3–4 tablespoons lemon juice

1 Lightly grease 4 large sheets of foil, each double-thickness. Mix together the herbs, peppercorns, juice and salt and pepper to taste in a bowl. Cut the lemon into 8 slices, then cut each slice in half. Place 4 lemon pieces in each fish cavity. Spoon the herb mixture into the fish cavities.

2 Place each fish on a piece of foil and sprinkle each with 1 tablespoon of wine. Seal the fish in the foil to form neat parcels. Cook on a hot barbecue grill plate or flat plate for 10–15 minutes, or until the fish is just cooked through and can be gently flaked with a fork. Leave the fish to stand, still wrapped in foil, for 5 minutes, before serving.

3 To make the horseradish cream, mix together all the ingredients and then season well. Serve in a small bowl with the fish.

4 To make the lemon sauce, process the yolks in a food processor for 20 seconds, or until blended. With the motor running, add the butter slowly in a thin, steady stream. Continue processing until all the butter has been added and the sauce is thick and creamy. Add the juice and season with salt and pepper. Serve in a small bowl with the fish.

NUTRITION PER SERVE
Protein 33 g; Fat 58 g; Carbohydrate 4 g; Dietary Fibre 1 g; Cholesterol 334 mg; 2869 kJ (685 Cal)

Mix together the herbs, peppercorns, juice and salt and pepper and use to stuff the fish.

Sprinkle each fish with a tablespoon of wine and then wrap up in foil.

Make the lemon sauce in a food processor, adding the butter in a slow stream.

Scallops with sesame bok choy

PREPARATION TIME: 10 MINUTES + 15 MINUTES MARINATING | TOTAL COOKING TIME: 10 MINUTES | SERVES 4

24 large scallops with roe
2 tablespoons light soy sauce
1 tablespoon fish sauce
1 tablespoon honey
1 tablespoon kecap manis or soy sauce
    (see NOTE, page 30)
grated zest and juice of 1 lime
2 teaspoons grated fresh ginger
lime wedges, to serve

SESAME BOK CHOY
1 tablespoon sesame oil
1 tablespoon sesame seeds
1 garlic clove, crushed
8 baby bok choy (pak choy),
    halved lengthways

1 Rinse the scallops, remove the dark veins and dry with paper towels. Mix the light soy and fish sauces, honey, kecap manis or soy sauce, lime zest and juice and ginger. Pour over the scallops, cover and refrigerate for 15 minutes. Drain, reserving the marinade.

2 To make the sesame bok choy, pour the oil onto a hot barbecue grill plate or flat plate and add the sesame seeds and garlic. Cook, stirring, for 1 minute, or until the seeds are golden. Arrange the bok choy in a single layer on the hotplate and pour over the reserved marinade. Cook for 3–4 minutes, turning once, until tender. Remove and keep warm.

3 Wipe clean the hotplate, brush with oil and reheat. Add the scallops and cook, turning, for about 2 minutes, or until they become opaque. Serve on top of the bok choy, with the lime wedges.

Rinse the scallops and then remove their dark veins and dry with paper towels.

Arrange the halved bok choy in a single layer on the hotplate.

NUTRITION PER SERVE
Protein 15 g; Fat 5 g; Carbohydrate 10 g; Dietary Fibre 1 g; Cholesterol 25 mg; 670 kJ (160 Cal)

Stuffed squid tubes

PREPARATION TIME: 30 MINUTES | TOTAL COOKING TIME: 10 MINUTES | SERVES 4

8 very small squid tubes (see NOTE)
2 tablespoons oil
4 garlic cloves, chopped
2 lemongrass stems, finely chopped
4 coriander (cilantro) roots, chopped
1–2 teaspoons Thai green curry paste
125 g (4½ oz) minced (ground) pork
100 g (3½ oz) minced (ground) chicken
2 tablespoons fish sauce
2 tablespoons rice flour
1 tablespoon soy sauce
2 teaspoons soft brown sugar
chilli sauce, to serve

1 Pull the tentacles from the body of the squid and discard. Pull the quill from the pouch of the squid and discard. Pull the skin away from the flesh and discard it. Wash the tubes thoroughly.

2 Heat half the oil in a frying pan over medium heat. Add the garlic, lemongrass, coriander root and curry paste and stir-fry for 2 minutes. Remove from the heat; add the minced pork and chicken, the fish sauce and rice flour and mix well.

3 Fill each tube with the mixture and secure the end with a toothpick. Mix together the soy sauce, sugar and 1 tablespoon water and brush over the tubes.

4 Brush a barbecue grill plate or flat plate with the remaining oil and then heat to very hot. Add the tubes and cook, turning frequently, for 4–6 minutes, or until just firm to the touch. Leave for 2 minutes before slicing, or serve whole. Serve with chilli sauce.

NOTE: Don't use pre-cleaned squid, as the tip will have been removed and the stuffing will come out. Baby squid is very tender and only about 8 cm (3¼ inches) long.

NUTRITION PER SERVE
Protein 74 g; Fat 15 g; Carbohydrate 9 g; Dietary
Fibre 1 g; Cholesterol 744 mg; 1974 kJ (472 Cal)

Hold one end of the squid, pull the skin away from the flesh and discard it.

Secure the ends of the filled squid tubes with toothpicks so the filling won't come out.

Tuna with Mediterranean vegetables

PREPARATION TIME: 15 MINUTES + 30 MINUTES MARINATING | TOTAL COOKING TIME: 20 MINUTES | SERVES 4

185 ml (6 fl oz/¾ cup) olive oil

3 garlic cloves, crushed

2 tablespoons sweet chilli sauce

1 red capsicum (pepper), cut into
    bite-sized pieces

1 yellow capsicum (pepper), cut into bite-
    sized pieces

2 large zucchini (courgettes), thickly sliced

2 slender eggplants (aubergines), thickly
    sliced

olive oil, extra, for brushing

4 tuna steaks

LEMON AND CAPER MAYONNAISE

1 egg yolk

1 teaspoon grated lemon zest

2 tablespoons lemon juice

1 garlic clove, chopped

185 ml (6 fl oz/¾ cup) olive oil

1 tablespoon baby capers

1 Combine the olive oil, garlic and sweet chilli sauce in a large bowl. Add the capsicum, zucchini and eggplant, toss well, then marinate for 30 minutes.

2 For the mayonnaise, process the egg yolk, lemon zest, lemon juice and garlic together in a food processor until smooth. With the motor running, gradually add the oil in a thin steady stream until the mixture thickens and is a creamy consistency. Stir in the capers and ½ teaspoon salt. Set aside.

3 Cook the drained vegetables on a hot, lightly oiled barbecue grill plate or flat plate for 4–5 minutes each side, or until cooked through. Keep warm.

4 Brush the tuna steaks with the extra oil and barbecue for 2–3 minutes each side, or until just cooked (tuna should be rare in the centre). Serve the vegetables and tuna steaks with the lemon and caper mayonnaise.

VARIATION: *This recipe is also suitable for use with Atlantic salmon or swordfish.*

NUTRITION PER SERVE
Protein 68 g; Fat 69 g; Carbohydrate 6 g; Dietary Fibre 3 g; Cholesterol 151 mg; 3885 kJ (925 Cal)

Process the mayonnaise ingredients until smooth and creamy.

Turn the vegetables over when browned on one side, then cook through.

Garlic prawns

PREPARATION TIME: 10 MINUTES + 2 HOURS MARINATING | TOTAL COOKING TIME: 5 MINUTES | SERVES 4

500 g (1 lb 2 oz) raw king prawns (shrimp)

MARINADE
2 tablespoons lemon juice
2 tablespoons sesame oil
2 garlic cloves, crushed
2 teaspoons grated fresh ginger

1 Peel and devein the prawns, leaving the tails intact. Make a cut along the back of the prawn, slicing three-quarters of the way through the flesh from head to tail. Put the prawns in a non-metallic dish or bowl.

2 To make the marinade, mix together the lemon juice, oil, garlic and ginger and pour over the prawns. Cover and refrigerate for 2 hours.

3 Cook the prawns on a hot, lightly oiled barbecue grill plate or flat plate for 3–5 minutes, or until pink and cooked through. Brush frequently with the marinade while cooking and then serve immediately.

STORAGE: *Prawns should always be cooked and eaten within 24 hours of purchase.*

VARIATION: *For a stronger flavour, double the quantity of garlic and omit the ginger.*

NUTRITION PER SERVE
Protein 26 g; Fat 10 g; Carbohydrate 0.5 g; Dietary Fibre 0 g; Cholesterol 186 mg; 834 kJ (199 Cal)

Peel and devein the prawns, leaving their tails intact. Then make cuts in the bodies.

Put the prawns in a non-metallic dish to marinate so that the lemon juice doesn't react with the metal.

Cook the prawns on a hot, lightly greased barbecue until they are pink.

Thai baby octopus

PREPARATION TIME: 1 HOUR | TOTAL COOKING TIME: 15–25 MINUTES | SERVES 6

500 g (1 lb 2 oz) baby octopus
2 tablespoons oil
3 garlic cloves, chopped
1 tablespoon green or pink peppercorns
2–4 small red chillies, finely chopped
1 tablespoon fish sauce

1 Cut off the octopus heads, below the eyes, with a sharp knife. Discard the heads and guts. Push the beaks out with your index finger, remove and discard. Wash the octopus thoroughly under running water and drain on crumpled paper towels. If the octopus tentacles are large, cut into quarters. Put in a shallow dish.

2 Mix together the oil, garlic, peppercorns and chilli, add to the octopus and marinate for 30 minutes. Cook 3 octopus at a time, turning frequently, on a very hot, lightly oiled barbecue grill plate or flat plate for 3 minutes, or until they turn white. Do not overcook. Sprinkle the fish sauce over the top and serve immediately.

HINT: *This recipe is also suitable for squid. Wash the tubes, pat dry and cut into strips before marinating and cooking in the same way.*

NUTRITION PER SERVE
Protein 14 g; Fat 7 g; Carbohydrate 0 g; Dietary
Fibre 0 g; Cholesterol 166 mg; 522 kJ (125 Cal)

Use a sharp knife to slice off the head of the octopus so you can remove the gut.

Use your index finger to push the beak up so you can remove it.

Cook the octopus, turning frequently, until the flesh turns white.

Squid rings with salsa verde

PREPARATION TIME: 30 MINUTES + 30 MINUTES MARINATING | TOTAL COOKING TIME: 15 MINUTES | SERVES 4

1 kg (2 lb 4 oz) squid
250 ml (9 fl oz/1 cup) olive oil
2 tablespoons lemon juice
2 garlic cloves, crushed
2 tablespoons chopped oregano
2 tablespoons chopped flat-leaf (Italian)
    parsley
lemon wedges, to serve

SALSA VERDE
2 anchovy fillets, drained
1 tablespoon capers
1 garlic clove, crushed
2 tablespoons chopped flat-leaf (Italian)
    parsley
2 tablespoons olive oil

NUTRITION PER SERVE
Protein 42.5 g; Fat 72 g; Carbohydrate 0.5 g; Dietary
Fibre 0.5 g; Cholesterol 499 mg; 3404 kJ (813 Cal)

1 To clean the squid, hold onto the tube and gently pull the tentacles away from the head. Cut out the beak and discard with any intestines still attached to the tentacles. Rinse the tentacles in cold running water, pat dry and cut into 5 cm (2 inch) lengths. Place in a bowl. Clean out the tube cavity and remove the transparent backbone. Under cold running water, pull away the skin and discard. Rince the tube and dry well. Cut into rings and place in the bowl with the tentacles. Add the oil, lemon juice, garlic and oregano and toss to coat. Refrigerate for 30 minutes.

2 To make the salsa verde, crush the anchovy fillets in a mortar and pestle. Rinse and chop the capers very finely and mix with the anchovies. Add the garlic and parsley, then slowly stir in the olive oil. Season and mix well.

3 Drain the squid, reserving the marinade, and cook on a hot, lightly oiled barbecue grill plate or flat plate in batches for 1–2 minutes each side, basting with the marinade. To serve, sprinkle the squid with salt, pepper and parsley, and serve with the salsa verde and lemon wedges.

Hold the squid and gently pull the tentacles away from the head.

Mix together the crushed anchovies, capers, garlic and parsley.

Cook the squid in batches on a hot barbecue grill plate or flat plate.

Cajun-blackened fish with pineapple salsa

PREPARATION TIME: 15 MINUTES + 20 MINUTES REFRIGERATION | TOTAL COOKING TIME: 10 MINUTES | SERVES 6

8 cm (3¼ inch) piece fresh pineapple, finely diced
6 spring onions (scallions), thinly sliced
2 tablespoons finely shredded mint
60 ml (2 fl oz/¼ cup) white wine vinegar
2 tablespoons olive oil
6 tablespoons ready-made Cajun spices
6 firm white fish fillets, such as blue eye
60 g (2¼ oz/¼ cup) Greek-style yoghurt

1 Place the pineapple, spring onion and mint in a bowl. Season with pepper and mix together well. Just before serving, stir in the vinegar and olive oil.

2 Place the Cajun spices in a dry frying pan and dry-fry over medium heat for 1 minute, or until fragrant. Transfer the spices to a sheet of baking paper and lightly coat each side of the fish fillets, patting off any excess. Refrigerate for 20 minutes.

3 Cook the fish on a hot, lightly oiled barbecue grill plate or flat plate for 2–3 minutes on each side, depending on the thickness of the fish. Serve with a little yoghurt spooned over the top and the salsa on the side.

NUTRITION PER SERVE
Protein 15 g; Fat 12 g; Carbohydrate 8 g; Dietary Fibre 2 g; Cholesterol 47 mg; 883 kJ (199 Cal)

Mix together the pineapple, spring onion and mint and season with pepper.

Put the spices on a sheet of baking paper and lightly coat both sides of the fish.

Cook the fish for 2–3 minutes on each side, depending on its thickness.

Prawns with mango salsa

PREPARATION TIME: 25 MINUTES + 1 HOUR MARINATING | TOTAL COOKING TIME: 10 MINUTES | SERVES 4–6

1 kg (2 lb 4 oz) raw prawns (shrimp)
80 ml (2½ fl oz/⅓ cup) lemon juice
80 ml (2½ fl oz/⅓ cup) olive oil
4 tablespoons chopped dill
450 g (1 lb) mango, cubed
1 onion, finely diced
1 red chilli, seeded and finely chopped
1 tablespoon grated lemon zest

1 Peel and devein the prawns, keeping the tails intact.

2 Combine the lemon juice, olive oil, dill and a teaspoon of salt in a shallow, non-metallic dish, add the prawns and toss. Cover and refrigerate for 1 hour.

3 Drain the prawns, reserving the marinade, and cook on a very hot, lightly oiled barbecue grill or flat plate for 3 minutes, or until they change colour.

4 Put the reserved marinade in a saucepan on the stovetop or barbecue and boil for 5 minutes. Mix with the prawns.

5 Mix together the mango, onion, chilli, lemon zest and some salt and pepper. Add the prawns and toss together gently.

NUTRITION PER SERVE (6)
Protein 35 g; Fat 15 g; Carbohydrate 10 g; Dietary Fibre 2 g; Cholesterol 250 mg; 1320 kJ (315 Cal)

Peel the prawns and remove the veins from the prawn backs, leaving the tails intact.

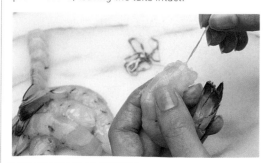

Cook the prawns on a very hot barbecue until they change colour.

Mix together the mango, onion, chilli, lemon zest and salt and pepper.

Fish wrapped in banana leaves

PREPARATION TIME: 20 MINUTES | TOTAL COOKING TIME: 35 MINUTES | SERVES 4–6

SPICE PASTE
1 red onion, finely chopped
3 small red chillies, seeded and chopped
1 teaspoon dried shrimp paste
1 cm (½ inch) piece galangal, finely chopped
1 lemongrass stem, white part only,
    finely sliced
5 blanched almonds, chopped
4 makrut (kaffir lime) leaves, finely shredded

2 teaspoons sesame oil
1 tablespoon vegetable oil
1 teaspoon soy sauce
1 banana leaf (about 50 x 30 cm/
    20 x 12 inches)
1 whole trout or silver bream (about 750 g/
    1 lb 10 oz), cleaned and scaled

1 To make the spice paste, grind all the ingredients except the makrut leaves in a food processor with 2 tablespoons water until smooth. Transfer to a bowl and mix in the makrut leaves. Set aside.

2 Heat the sesame oil and vegetable oil in a small frying pan and gently fry the paste for 5 minutes. Mix in the soy sauce. Remove from the heat and cool.

3 Cut a large rectangle from the banana leaf and brush with oil. Score the fish several times on both sides and rub in the paste, pushing it well into the cuts.

4 Place the fish on the banana leaf and fold over to make a parcel. Wrap again in foil to secure and protect. Cook over medium heat on a hot, lightly oiled barbecue grill plate or flat plate for 20–30 minutes, or until the flesh flakes easily when tested with a fork.

NUTRITION PER SERVE (6)
Protein 30 g; Fat 15 g; Carbohydrate 3 g; Dietary
Fibre 1 g; Cholesterol 75 mg; 1050 kJ (250 Cal)

Add the shredded makrut leaves to the smooth spice paste.

Score the fish several times on both sides with a sharp knife.

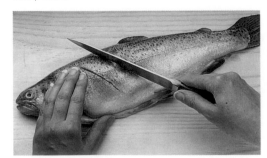

Wrap the fish in the banana leaf, folding the ends securely to make a parcel.

Sweet chilli octopus

PREPARATION TIME: 15 MINUTES | TOTAL COOKING TIME: 5 MINUTES | SERVES 4

1.5 kg (3 lb 5 oz) baby octopus
250 ml (9 fl oz/1 cup) sweet chilli sauce
80 ml (2½ fl oz/⅓ cup) lime juice
80 ml (2½ fl oz/⅓ cup) fish sauce
60 g (2¼ oz/⅓ cup) soft brown sugar
lime wedges, to serve

1 Cut off the octopus heads, below the eyes, with a sharp knife. Discard the heads and guts. Push the beaks out with your index finger, remove and discard. Wash the octopus thoroughly under running water and drain on crumpled paper towels. If the octopus tentacles are large, cut into quarters.

2 Mix together the sweet chilli sauce, lime juice, fish sauce and sugar.

3 Cook the octopus on a very hot, lightly oiled barbecue grill plate or flat plate, turning often, for 3–4 minutes, or until it just changes colour. Brush with a quarter of the sauce during cooking. Do not overcook the octopus or it will toughen. Serve immediately with the remaining sauce and lime wedges.

NUTRITION PER SERVE
Protein 43 g; Fat 11 g; Carbohydrate 25 g; Dietary Fibre 2.5 g; Cholesterol 500 mg; 1543 kJ (370 Cal)

Push the beak upwards with your index finger to remove it.

Mix together the sweet chilli sauce, lime juice, fish sauce and sugar.

Cook the octopus just until it changes colour, otherwise it will be tough.

Salmon cutlets with tropical fruit salsa

PREPARATION TIME: 20 MINUTES + AT LEAST 3 HOURS MARINATING | TOTAL COOKING TIME: 20 MINUTES | SERVES 4

4 salmon cutlets
1½ tablespoons seasoned pepper or cracked
    black pepper
2 tablespoons lemon juice
125 ml (4 fl oz/½ cup) lime juice
1 tablespoon chopped thyme

FRUIT SALSA
½ small papaya, peeled
¼ small pineapple, peeled
3 spring onions (scallions), chopped
1 tablespoon chopped coriander (cilantro)
2 tablespoons lime juice
3 teaspoons caster (superfine) sugar

1   Sprinkle the salmon all over with the seasoned pepper or cracked black pepper. Place in a shallow non-metallic dish. Mix together the lemon juice, lime juice and thyme and pour over the salmon. Cover and refrigerate for at least 3 hours.

2   To make the salsa, chop the papaya and pineapple into small dice. Mix with the spring onion, coriander, lime juice, caster sugar and season with salt.

3   Cook the salmon on a hot, lightly oiled barbecue grill plate or flat plate, brushing with any remaining marinade. Cook for 5–10 minutes each side, turning once, until lightly browned and the flesh is just cooked. Serve with the salsa.

STORAGE: *Do not marinate fish for more than 3 hours, as the citrus juices will begin to cook the fish and turn the flesh opaque. If this should occur, reduce the cooking time by half. Salsa should be made just before serving.*

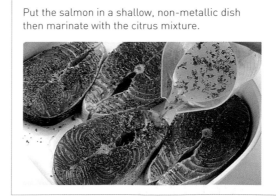

Put the salmon in a shallow, non-metallic dish then marinate with the citrus mixture.

Cook the salmon until it is lightly browned on the outside and the flesh is just cooked.

NUTRITION PER SERVE
Protein 20 g; Fat 12 g; Carbohydrate 13 g; Dietary Fibre 3 g; Cholesterol 70 mg; 980 kJ (235 Cal)

Malaysian barbecued seafood

PREPARATION TIME: 30 MINUTES + 15 MINUTES MARINATING | TOTAL COOKING TIME: 10 MINUTES | SERVES 6

1 onion, grated
4 garlic cloves, chopped
5 cm (2 inch) piece of fresh ginger, grated
3 lemongrass stems, white part only, chopped
2 teaspoons ground or grated fresh turmeric
1 teaspoon shrimp paste
80 ml (2½ fl oz/⅓ cup) vegetable oil
4 medium squid tubes
2 thick white boneless fish fillets
8 raw king prawns (shrimp)
2 limes, cut into wedges

1 Combine the onion, garlic, ginger, lemongrass, turmeric, shrimp paste, oil and ¼ teaspoon of salt in a small food processor. Process in short bursts until the mixture forms a paste.

2 Cut the squid in half lengthways and lay it on the work surface with the soft inside facing up. Score a very fine honeycomb pattern into the soft side, taking care not to cut all the way through, and then cut into large pieces. Wash all the seafood under cold running water and pat dry with paper towels. Brush the seafood lightly with the spice paste. Place the seafood on a tray, cover and refrigerate for 15 minutes.

3 Lightly oil a barbecue grill plate or flat plate and heat. When the plate is hot, arrange the fish fillets and prawns side by side on the plate. Cook for about 3 minutes on each side, turning them once only, or until the fish flesh is just firm and the prawns turn bright pink to orange. Add the squid pieces and cook for about 2 minutes, or until the flesh turns white and rolls up—take care not to overcook the seafood.

4 Arrange the seafood on a platter, add the lime wedges and serve immediately, garnished with strips of lime zest and some mint, if you like.

NUTRITION PER SERVE
Protein 33 g; Fat 3 g; Carbohydrate 1 g; Dietary Fibre 1 g; Cholesterol 300 mg; 681 kJ (163 Cal)

Process in short bursts until the mixture forms a paste for coating the seafood.

Score a fine honeycomb pattern into the soft underside of the squid.

Salmon with dill cream

PREPARATION TIME: 25 MINUTES | TOTAL COOKING TIME: 25 MINUTES | SERVES 4

4 small salmon
4 garlic cloves, peeled
2 lemons, sliced
8 fresh bay leaves
8 sprigs flat-leaf (Italian) parsley
8 sprigs thyme
olive oil, for brushing

DILL CREAM
90 g (3¼ oz) butter
250 ml (9 fl oz/1 cup) fish stock
1½ teaspoons wholegrain mustard
250 ml (9 fl oz/1 cup) pouring
   (whipping) cream
2 tablespoons lemon juice
3 tablespoons chopped dill

1   Wash the fish and pat dry inside and out with paper towels. Place a clove of garlic, a few slices of lemon and a bay leaf in the cavity of each fish. Bundle together a sprig of parsley and thyme and tie a bundle with string onto each fish, near the tail. Reserve the other sprigs. Brush both sides of the fish with a little of the olive oil.

2   For the dill cream, melt the butter in a saucepan and add the fish stock, mustard and cream. Bring to the boil, then reduce the heat and simmer for 15 minutes, or until the sauce is slightly thickened. Stir in the lemon juice and dill. Season and keep warm.

3   While the dill cream is cooking, cook the fish on a hot, lightly oiled barbecue grill plate or flat plate for 3–6 minutes on each side, turning carefully, or until cooked through. Discard the herbs. For serving, bundle together a parsley sprig, a thyme sprig and a bay leaf, and tie a bundle near each fish tail. Serve warm with the dill cream.

Wash the fish and pat dry inside and out with paper towels.

Tie together a sprig of parsley and a sprig of thyme and tie to the tail of the fish.

NUTRITION PER SERVE
Protein 52 g; Fat 78 g; Carbohydrate 1 g; Dietary
Fibre 0 g; Cholesterol 350 mg; 3860 kJ (920 Cal)

Garlic squid with parmesan

PREPARATION TIME: 30 MINUTES + AT LEAST 10 MINUTES MARINATING | TOTAL COOKING TIME: 5 MINUTES | SERVES 2–4 (SEE NOTE)

350 g (12 oz) squid tubes, cleaned
4 garlic cloves, chopped
2 tablespoons olive oil
2 tablespoons finely chopped parsley
1 large tomato, peeled, seeded and
    finely chopped
25 g (1 oz/¼ cup) grated parmesan cheese

1   Cut the squid tubes in half lengthways, wash and pat dry. Lay them flat, with the soft, fleshy underside facing upwards, and cut into rectangular pieces, about 6 x 2.5 cm (2½ x 1 inches). Finely honeycomb by scoring the fleshy side with diagonal strips, one way and then the other, to create a diamond pattern. Do not cut right through the flesh.

2   Mix the garlic, oil, half the parsley, and salt and pepper to taste in a bowl. Add the squid and refrigerate for at least 10 minutes.

3   Cook on a very hot, lightly oiled barbecue grill plate or flat plate in 2 batches, tossing regularly, until the squid just turns white (take care never to overcook squid or it can become tough). Add the chopped tomato and toss through to just heat.

4   Arrange the squid on a plate and scatter with the parmesan and remaining parsley.

NOTE: *This dish will serve four as a starter and two as a main course.*

NUTRITION PER SERVE (4)
Protein 20 g; Fat 15 g; Carbohydrate 2 g; Dietary Fibre 1 g; Cholesterol 180 mg; 800 kJ (190 Cal)

Honeycomb the soft fleshy side of the squid with a sharp knife.

Cook the squid in batches, tossing regularly, until it turns white.

Vegetables and salads

Chargrilled vegetables

PREPARATION TIME: 15 MINUTES + 40 MINUTES STANDING | TOTAL COOKING TIME: 40 MINUTES | SERVES 6

2 eggplants (aubergines)
900 g (2 lb) orange sweet potato
4 zucchini (courgettes)
2 red capsicums (peppers)
600 g (1 lb 5 oz) button mushrooms
80 ml (2½ fl oz/⅓ cup) olive oil

BASIL DRESSING
125 ml (4 fl oz/½ cup) olive oil
2 garlic cloves, crushed
2 tablespoons balsamic vinegar
½ teaspoon sugar
1 large handful basil

NUTRITION PER SERVE
Protein 9 g; Fat 20 g; Carbohydrate 28 g; Dietary
Fibre 9 g; Cholesterol 0 mg; 1495 kJ (355 Cal)

1 Cut the eggplant into 1 cm (½ inch) thick slices. Place on a wire rack and sprinkle liberally with salt. Leave for 30 minutes, then rinse under cold water and pat dry with paper towels.

2 Cut the sweet potato into 5 mm (¼ inch) slices and the zucchini into 1 cm (½ inch) slices. Quarter the capsicums, remove the seeds and membranes and put on a hot, lightly oiled barbecue grill plate or flat plate, skin side down, until the skin blackens and blisters. Place in a plastic bag and leave to cool. Peel away the skin.

3 Brush the eggplant, sweet potato, zucchini and mushrooms with oil. Cook on a hot, lightly oiled barbecue grill plate or flat plate in batches until lightly browned and cooked through.

4 To make the basil dressing, put the oil, garlic, vinegar, sugar and basil in a food processor or blender and process until smooth.

5 Toss the vegetables with the basil dressing. Allow to cool, then cover and refrigerate until ready to use. Return to room temperature before serving.

Put the slices of eggplant on a wire rack and sprinkle with salt.

Use a sharp knife to cut the sweet potato into thin slices.

Once cooled, gently peel the blackened skin off the capsicums.

Ham and herb mushrooms

PREPARATION TIME: 15 MINUTES | TOTAL COOKING TIME: 5 MINUTES | SERVES 8

8 large flat field mushrooms
3 spring onions (scallions), finely chopped
150 g (5½ oz) smoked ham, finely chopped
60 g (2¼ oz/¾ cup) fresh breadcrumbs
2 tablespoons finely grated parmesan cheese
1 tablespoon chopped parsley
2 teaspoons chopped oregano
2 tablespoons olive oil

1 Remove the stalks from the mushrooms and finely chop the stalks. Mix the mushroom stalks with the spring onion, ham, breadcrumbs, parmesan cheese, parsley and oregano. Season with salt and black pepper and add a little water to bring the mixture together.

2 Divide the mixture among the mushroom caps and brush lightly with the olive oil.

3 Cook on a hot, lightly oiled barbecue grill plate or flat plate, filling side up, for about 3 minutes. Cover loosely with foil and steam for another 2 minutes.

NOTE: *Serve as a main course with bread or as a side dish with barbecued meats. For vegetarian mushrooms, use feta cheese instead of ham.*

NUTRITION PER SERVE
Protein 7 g; Fat 5 g; Carbohydrate 6 g; Dietary Fibre 1 g; Cholesterol 10 mg; 415 kJ (98 Cal)

Remove the stalks from the mushrooms and leave the mushroom caps for filling.

Finely chop the mushroom stalks to mix with the other filling ingredients.

Spoon the filling into the mushroom caps and then brush lightly with oil.

Barbecued corn in the husk

PREPARATION TIME: 15 MINUTES I TOTAL COOKING TIME: 40 MINUTES I SERVES 8

8 fresh young corn cobs
125 ml (4 fl oz/½ cup) olive oil
6 garlic cloves, chopped
4 tablespoons chopped parsley

1 Peel back the corn husks, leaving them intact. Pull off the white silks and discard. Wash the corn and pat dry with paper towels.

2 Combine the olive oil, garlic, parsley and some salt and black pepper and brush over each cob. Pull up the husks and tie together at the top with string. Steam over boiling water for 20 minutes, then pat dry.

3 Cook on a hot, lightly oiled barbecue grill plate or flat plate for 20 minutes, turning regularly. Spray with water during the cooking to keep the corn moist.

NUTRITION PER SERVE
Protein 3 g; Fat 15 g; Carbohydrate 15 g; Dietary Fibre 3 g; Cholesterol 0 mg; 860 kJ (205 Cal)

Carefully peel back the corn husks, then pull away the white silks (threads) and wash the corn.

Brush the oil, garlic, parsley and seasoning over the corn, then pull up the husk.

Tie the tops of the husks in place with kitchen string so they are secure.

Potato and tomato gratin

PREPARATION TIME: 15 MINUTES | TOTAL COOKING TIME: 1 HOUR 15 MINUTES | SERVES 8

1.5 kg (3 lb 5 oz) potatoes
40 g (1½ oz) butter, melted
1 tablespoon chopped herbs
    (such as thyme, marjoram, parsley,
    rosemary and oregano)
310 ml (10¾ fl oz/1¼ cups) pouring
    (whipping) cream
2 ripe tomatoes, thinly sliced
40 g (1½ oz/½ cup) fresh breadcrumbs
125 g (4½ oz/1 cup) grated cheddar cheese
1 tablespoon snipped chives

NUTRITION PER SERVE
Protein 14 g; Fat 32 g; Carbohydrate 30 g; Dietary
Fibre 4 g; Cholesterol 99 mg; 1960 kJ (468 Cal)

1   Preheat the oven to 180°C (350°F/ Gas 4). Peel and thinly slice the potatoes. Brush a shallow baking dish with butter and arrange the potatoes in overlapping layers.

2   Scatter on the herbs, pepper and salt and pour the cream into the centre of the dish. Cover with foil and bake for 1 hour. (The dish can now be removed from the oven, allowed to cool, then refrigerated for later.)

3   Increase the oven to 210°C (415°F/ Gas 6–7). Arrange the tomato over the potato. Scatter evenly with the combined breadcrumbs and cheese and return to the oven. Bake, uncovered, for 15 minutes, or until golden on top. Sprinkle with the snipped chives and serve immediately.

VARIATION: *Thinly slice an onion and layer alternately with the potato.*

Peel the potatoes and thinly slice them, then arrange in the dish.

Scatter the herbs, pepper and salt over the potato and pour the cream in the centre.

Arrange the tomato slices over the cooked potato and sprinkle with breadcrumbs and cheese.

Grilled haloumi and roast vegetable salad

PREPARATION TIME: 15 MINUTES | TOTAL COOKING TIME: 30 MINUTES | SERVES 4

4 slender eggplants (aubergines), cut in half
    and then halved lengthways
1 red capsicum (pepper), halved,
    thickly sliced
4 small zucchini (courgettes), cut in half
    widthways and then halved lengthways
80 ml (2½ fl oz/⅓ cup) olive oil
2 garlic cloves, crushed
200 g (7 oz) haloumi cheese, thinly sliced
150 g (5½ oz) baby English spinach
    leaves, trimmed
1 tablespoon balsamic vinegar

1   Preheat the oven to 220°C (425°F/
Gas 7). Place the vegetables in a large bowl,
add 60 ml (2 fl oz/¼ cup) of the olive oil and
the garlic, season and toss well to combine.
Place the vegetables in an ovenproof dish in
a single layer. Roast for 20–30 minutes, or until
tender and browned around the edges.

2   Meanwhile, cook the haloumi slices on
a hot, lightly oiled barbecue grill plate or flat
plate for 1–2 minutes each side.

3   Top the spinach with the roast vegetables
and haloumi. Whisk together the remaining
oil and vinegar to make a dressing.

NUTRITION PER SERVE
Protein 14 g; Fat 28 g; Carbohydrate 6 g; Dietary
Fibre 5 g; Cholesterol 26 mg; 1383 kJ (330 Cal)

Roast the vegetables in a single layer until they are
tender and browned at the edges.

Cook the haloumi on a lightly oiled barbecue grill
plate or flat plate for 1–2 minutes on each side.

Mix the remaining oil with the vinegar to make a
dressing for the salad.

Chargrilled asparagus

PREPARATION TIME: 5 MINUTES | TOTAL COOKING TIME: 3 MINUTES | SERVES 4

500 g (1 lb 2 oz) asparagus
2 garlic cloves, crushed
2 tablespoons balsamic vinegar
2 tablespoons olive oil
50 g (1¼ oz) parmesan cheese shavings

1 Break off the woody ends from the asparagus by gently bending the stems until the tough end snaps away. Cook the asparagus on a hot, lightly oiled barbecue grill plate or flat plate for 3 minutes, or until bright green and tender.

2 To make the dressing, whisk together the garlic, vinegar and olive oil.

3 Pour the dressing over the warm asparagus and top with the parmesan shavings and lots of black pepper, if desired.

NUTRITION PER SERVE
Protein 8 g; Fat 15 g; Carbohydrate 2 g; Dietary Fibre 2 g; Cholesterol 10 mg; 700 kJ (165 Cal)

To break the woody ends from the asparagus, hold both ends and bend gently.

Cook the asparagus on a hot barbecue grill plate or flat plate until it is bright green and tender.

The easiest way to make parmesan shavings is to run a potato peeler over the block of cheese.

Roasted balsamic onions

PREPARATION TIME: 15 MINUTES + OVERNIGHT REFRIGERATION I TOTAL COOKING TIME: 1 HOUR 30 MINUTES I SERVES 8

1 kg (2 lb 4 oz) pickling onions, unpeeled
(see NOTE)
185 ml (6 fl oz/¾ cup) balsamic vinegar
2 tablespoons soft brown sugar
185 ml (6 fl oz/¾ cup) olive oil

1 Preheat the oven to 160°C (315°F/ Gas 2–3). Place the unpeeled onions in a baking dish and roast for 1½ hours. Leave until cool enough to handle. Trim the stems from the onions and peel away the skin (the outer part of the root should come away, but the onions will remain intact). Rinse a 1 litre (35 fl oz/4 cups) wide-necked jar with boiling water and dry in a warm oven—do not dry with a tea towel (dish towel). Put the onions in the jar.

2 Combine the vinegar and sugar in a small screw-top jar and stir to dissolve the sugar. Add the oil, seal the jar and shake vigorously until combined—the mixture will become paler and may separate on standing.

3 Pour the vinegar mixture over the onions, seal, and turn upside down to coat. Marinate overnight in the refrigerator, turning occasionally. Return to room temperature and shake before serving.

NOTE: *Pickling onions are very small, usually packed in 1 kg (2 lb 4 oz) bags. The ideal size is around 35 g (1¼ oz) each. The sizes in the bag will probably range from 20 g (¾ oz) up to 40 g (1½ oz). The cooking time given is suitable for this range and there is no need to cook the larger ones for any longer. The marinating time given is a minimum time and the onions may be marinated for up to 3 days in the refrigerator. The marinade may separate after a few hours, which is fine; simply stir occasionally.*

NUTRITION PER SERVE
Protein 0.5 g; Fat 7.5 g; Carbohydrate 20 g;
Dietary Fibre 2 g; Cholesterol 0 mg; 677 kJ (162 Cal)

When cool, trim the stems from the onions and peel away the skin.

Add the oil to the vinegar and sugar and shake vigorously to combine.

Pour the vinegar mixture over the onions, turning the jar to coat thoroughly.

Chargrilled potatoes with pistachio salsa

PREPARATION TIME: 25 MINUTES I TOTAL COOKING TIME: 20 MINUTES I SERVES 4

PISTACHIO SALSA
150 g (5½ oz) pistachio nuts, toasted
2 ripe tomatoes, chopped
2 garlic cloves, finely chopped
1 small red chilli, finely chopped
2 tablespoons chopped parsley
1 tablespoon chopped mint
1 teaspoon finely grated lemon zest

750 g (1 lb 10 oz) potatoes
3 tablespoons plain (all-purpose) flour
2 tablespoons olive oil
sour cream, to serve

1 To make the pistachio salsa, roughly chop the nuts and combine with the tomato, garlic, chilli, herbs and lemon zest. Season with salt and pepper.

2 Peel the potatoes and cut into large wedges. Place in a saucepan and cover with water, bring to the boil and cook for 5 minutes. Transfer to a colander and rinse under running water to stop the cooking. Pat the wedges dry with paper towels.

3 Sprinkle the flour over the potatoes in a bowl and toss to lightly coat. Cook the potato wedges in a single layer on a hot, lightly oiled barbecue grill plate or flat plate for 5–10 minutes, or until golden brown and tender. Drizzle with the olive oil and turn the potatoes regularly during cooking. Serve with the salsa and a bowl of sour cream.

To make the salsa, simply mix together all the ingredients and season well.

Cook the potato wedges on the barbecue until they are golden brown.

NUTRITION PER SERVE
Protein 10 g; Fat 30 g; Carbohydrate 30 g; Dietary Fibre 5 g; Cholesterol 0 mg; 1755 kJ (415 Cal)

Barbecued baby potatoes

PREPARATION TIME: 20 MINUTES + 1 HOUR STANDING | TOTAL COOKING TIME: 20 MINUTES | SERVES 6

750 g (1 lb 10 oz) baby potatoes, unpeeled
2 tablespoons olive oil
2 tablespoons thyme
sea salt, to serve

1 Cut any large potatoes in half so that they are all the same size for even cooking. Boil, steam or microwave the potatoes until just tender. Drain and lightly dry with paper towels.

2 Put the potatoes in a large bowl and add the oil and thyme. Toss gently and leave for 1 hour.

3 Drain potatoes, reserving oil mixture. Cook the potatoes on a hot, lightly oiled barbecue grill plate or flat plate for 15 minutes, turning frequently and brushing with the remaining oil and thyme mixture, until golden brown. Sprinkle with 2 teaspoons crushed sea salt to serve.

NOTE: *The potatoes can be left in the marinade for up to 2 hours before barbecuing, but should be served immediately after they are cooked.*

NUTRITION PER SERVE
Protein 3 g; Fat 7 g; Carbohydrate 16 g; Dietary
Fibre 2 g; Cholesterol 0 mg; 576 kJ (138 Cal)

Boil, steam or microwave the potatoes until they are just tender but still whole.

Toss the potatoes with the oil and thyme and then leave for an hour.

While the potatoes are cooking, turn and brush them frequently with the oil and thyme.

Chickpea salad

PREPARATION TIME: 20 MINUTES | TOTAL COOKING TIME: NIL | SERVES 8

2 large tins chickpeas (see NOTE)
3 tomatoes
1 red onion, thinly sliced
1 small red capsicum (pepper), cut into
thin strips
4 spring onions (scallions), cut into thin strips
3 very large handfuls chopped parsley
2–3 tablespoons chopped mint

DRESSING
2 tablespoons tahini (sesame paste)
2 tablespoons fresh lemon juice
3 tablespoons olive oil
2 garlic cloves, crushed
½ teaspoon ground cumin

1 Drain the chickpeas and rinse well. Cut the tomatoes in half and remove the seeds with a spoon. Dice the flesh. Mix the onion, tomato, capsicum and spring onion in a bowl. Add the chickpeas, parsley and mint.

2 To make the dressing, put all the ingredients in a screw-top jar with 2 tablespoons water, season well and shake vigorously to make a creamy liquid. Pour over the salad and toss.

STORAGE: *Can be kept, covered, in the fridge for up to 3 hours.*

NOTE: *You can also use dried chickpeas, but they will need to be soaked and cooked first. Use 380 g (13½ oz/1¾ cups) dried chickpeas and put in a saucepan with 3.5 litres (122 fl oz/ 14 cups) water and 3 tablespoons olive oil. Partially cover and boil for 2½ hours, or until tender. Rinse, drain well and allow to cool a little before making the salad.*

NUTRITION PER SERVE
Protein 4 g; Fat 2 g; Carbohydrate 8 g; Dietary
Fibre 3 g; Cholesterol 0 mg; 877 kJ (210 Cal)

Both tinned and dried chickpeas should be rinsed and drained well.

Cut the tomatoes in half and scoop out the seeds with a teaspoon.

The easiest way to make a salad dressing is by shaking the ingredients in a screw-top jar.

Tomato and bocconcini salad

PREPARATION TIME: **10** MINUTES | TOTAL COOKING TIME: NIL | SERVES 4

3 large vine-ripened tomatoes
250 g (9 oz) bocconcini or mozzarella cheese
12 basil leaves
3 tablespoons extra virgin olive oil

1 Slice the tomatoes thickly (you will need roughly 12 slices). Slice the bocconcini into about 24 slices.

2 Arrange the tomato slices on a serving plate, alternating them with 2 slices of bocconcini. Place the basil leaves between the bocconcini slices.

3 Drizzle with the oil and season well with salt and ground black pepper.

NOTE: *Bocconcini are fresh baby mozzarella. Use very fresh buffalo mozzarella, if you can find it.*

Slice the bocconcini or mozzarella into about 24 fairly thick slices.

Arrange the tomato slices on a serving plate, alternating with the bocconcini.

NUTRITION PER SERVE
Protein 14 g; Fat 25 g; Carbohydrate 3 g; Dietary Fibre 1 g; Cholesterol 33 mg; 1221 kJ (292 Cal)

Semi-dried tomato and baby spinach salad

PREPARATION TIME: 15 MINUTES | TOTAL COOKING TIME: NIL | SERVES 6

2 quarters preserved lemon (see NOTE)
150 g (5½ oz) baby English spinach leaves
200 g (7 oz) sliced semi-dried (sun-blushed)
    tomatoes
225 g (8 oz) jar drained and sliced marinated
    artichoke hearts
90 g (3¼ oz/¾ cup) small pitted black olives
2 tablespoons lemon juice
3 tablespoons olive oil
1 large garlic clove, crushed

1   Remove and discard the pith and flesh
from the preserved lemon. Wash the zest and
thinly slice.

2   Place the spinach in a bowl with the
semi-dried tomatoes, artichoke hearts, olives
and preserved lemon.

3   Whisk together the lemon juice, olive oil and
garlic, season and pour over the salad. Toss and
serve immediately.

NOTE: *Preserved lemon can be bought in jars
from delicatessens and speciality food stores. Only
the zest is used; discard the pith and flesh.*

NUTRITION PER SERVE
Protein 3 g; Fat 13 g; Carbohydrate 10.5 g; Dietary
Fibre 2.7 g; Cholesterol 0 mg; 746 kJ (178 Cal)

Remove and discard the pith from the preserved
lemon. Wash the zest and thinly slice.

Curly endive with crisp prosciutto and garlic croutons

PREPARATION TIME: 20 MINUTES | TOTAL COOKING TIME: 5 MINUTES | SERVES 6

1 large bunch curly endive
½ red oak leaf lettuce
2 red onions
4 slices white or wholemeal (whole-wheat) bread
2 large garlic cloves, crushed
60 g (2¼ oz) butter, softened
30 g (1 oz) feta cheese, mashed
4–6 thin slices prosciutto
1 large avocado

DRESSING
2 tablespoons olive oil
3 tablespoons sugar
3 tablespoons tomato sauce (ketchup)
1 tablespoon soy sauce
80 ml (2½ fl oz/⅓ cup) red wine vinegar

1 Tear the endive and lettuce into pieces. Peel and slice the onions and separate into rings. Toss the endive, lettuce and onion in a salad bowl.

2 Toast the bread on one side only. Mash the garlic, butter and feta cheese into a paste and spread over the untoasted side of the bread. Remove the crusts and toast the buttered side of the bread until crisp and golden. Cut into small cubes.

3 Crisp the prosciutto under a very hot grill (broiler) for a few seconds. Remove and cut into pieces. Cut the avocado into thin wedges.

4 To make the dressing, whisk the oil, sugar, tomato sauce, soy sauce and vinegar together. Add the prosciutto and avocado to the salad and pour over half the dressing. Arrange the croutons on top and serve the remaining dressing on the side.

NUTRITION PER SERVE
Protein 5 g; Fat 24 g; Carbohydrate 22 g; Dietary Fibre 2 g; Cholesterol 27 mg; 1356 kJ (324 Cal)

Peel the red onion, slice it thinly and then separate into rings.

Spread the feta, butter and garlic paste over the untoasted side of the bread.

Crisp the prosciutto under a hot grill (broiler) and then cut it into pieces.

Couscous salad

PREPARATION TIME: 20 MINUTES | TOTAL COOKING TIME: 10 MINUTES | SERVES 6

500 g (1 lb 2 oz) couscous
1 red onion, chopped
200 g (7 oz) feta cheese, diced
40 g (1½ oz) black olives, sliced
2 Lebanese (short) cucumbers, peeled, seeded
  and chopped
3 very large handfuls mint, chopped
125 ml (4 fl oz/½ cup) olive oil
125 ml (4 fl oz/½ cup) lemon juice

1 Prepare the couscous according to the instructions on the packet.

2 Place in a large bowl with the onion, feta cheese, olives, cucumber and mint.

3 Whisk together the olive oil and lemon juice and toss through.

Prepare the couscous according to the instructions on the packet.

To make a dressing, whisk together the olive oil and lemon juice.

NUTRITION PER SERVE
Protein 17.5 g; Fat 27.5 g; Carbohydrate 68 g; Dietary
Fibre 2.1 g; Cholesterol 23 mg; 2494 kJ (596 Cal)

Feta, beetroot and rocket salad

PREPARATION TIME: 10 MINUTES | TOTAL COOKING TIME: NIL | SERVES 6

2 x 340 g (11¾ oz) tins baby beetroot (beets)
200 g (7 oz) baby rocket (arugula)
300 g (10½ oz) marinated feta, cubed
3 tablespoons olive oil
1 tablespoon balsamic vinegar

1   Drain the beetroot and cut into quarters.

2   Place in a large serving bowl with the rocket leaves and feta.

3   Whisk together the olive oil and balsamic vinegar, then pour over the salad and toss well. Season with black pepper.

NUTRITION PER SERVE
Protein 10.6 g; Fat 24.7 g; Carbohydrate 9.7 g; Dietary Fibre 2.7 g; Cholesterol 2 mg; 1277 kJ (305 Cal)

Whisk the olive oil and vinegar together. Pour the dressing over the salad and toss well.

Tabouleh

PREPARATION TIME: 20 MINUTES + 2 HOURS SOAKING AND DRYING | TOTAL COOKING TIME: NIL | SERVES 6

120 g (4¼ oz/¾ cup) burghul (bulgur)
3 ripe tomatoes
1 telegraph (long) cucumber
4 spring onions (scallions), sliced
120 g (4¼ oz/1 bunch) chopped flat-leaf
    (Italian) parsley
1 very large handful mint, chopped

DRESSING
80 ml (2½ fl oz/⅓ cup) lemon juice
3 tablespoons olive oil
1 tablespoon extra virgin olive oil

1 Place the burghul in a bowl, cover with 500 ml (17 fl oz/2 cups) water and leave for 1 hour 30 minutes.

2 Cut the tomatoes in half and remove the seeds with a spoon. Dice the flesh. Cut the cucumber in half lengthways, remove the seeds with a teaspoon and dice the flesh.

3 To make the dressing, whisk the lemon juice and 1½ teaspoons salt. Slowly whisk in the olive oil and extra virgin olive oil. Season with pepper.

4 Drain the burghul and squeeze out any excess water. Spread on paper towels and leave to dry for 30 minutes. Mix with the tomato, cucumber, spring onion and herbs. Add the dressing and toss together well.

NUTRITION PER SERVE
Protein 4 g; Fat 13 g; Carbohydrate 22 g; Dietary
Fibre 3.5 g; Cholesterol 0 mg; 950 kJ (227 Cal)

Whisk the olive oil and extra virgin olive oil into the lemon juice.

Drain the burghul and squeeze out any excess water, then spread on paper towels to dry.

Toss the salad ingredients together before adding the dressing.

Bean salad

PREPARATION TIME: 10 MINUTES | TOTAL COOKING TIME: 2 MINUTES | SERVES 6

250 g (9 oz) green beans
250 g (9 oz) yellow beans
3 tablespoons olive oil
1 tablespoon lemon juice
1 garlic clove, crushed
parmesan cheese shavings

1 Bring a saucepan of lightly salted water to the boil. Add the green and yellow beans and cook for 2 minutes, or until just tender. Plunge into cold water and leave in the water for 3 minutes to chill, then drain.

2 Whisk together the oil, lemon juice and garlic and season well.

3 Place the beans in a serving bowl, pour on the dressing and toss to coat. Top with parmesan shavings and serve immediately.

NUTRITION PER SERVE
Protein 2.8 g; Fat 10.1 g; Carbohydrate 2.1 g; Dietary Fibre 2.3 g; Cholesterol 2 mg; 481 kJ (115 Cal)

Whisk together the oil, lemon juice and garlic to emulsify.

Roast tomato salad

PREPARATION TIME: 10 MINUTES | TOTAL COOKING TIME: 5 MINUTES | SERVES 6

6 roma (plum) tomatoes
2 teaspoons capers
6 basil leaves, torn
1 tablespoon olive oil
1 tablespoon balsamic vinegar
2 garlic cloves, crushed
½ teaspoon honey

1 Cut the tomatoes into quarters lengthways. Cook, skin side down, on a hot barbecue grill plate or flat plate or under a kitchen grill (broiler) for 4–5 minutes, or until golden. Cool to room temperature.

2 Combine the capers, basil, oil, vinegar, garlic and honey in a bowl, season with salt and freshly ground black pepper, and pour over the tomatoes. Toss gently.

NUTRITION PER SERVE
Protein 1.1 g; Fat 3.2 g; Carbohydrate 2.6 g; Dietary Fibre 1.4 g; Cholesterol 0 mg; 196 kJ (47 Cal)

Cook the tomato quarters for 4–5 minutes, or until golden.

Stir-fried salad

PREPARATION TIME: 20 MINUTES | TOTAL COOKING TIME: 10 MINUTES | SERVES 6

1 red capsicum (pepper)
100 g (3½ oz) oyster mushrooms
425 g (15 oz) tin baby corn
500 g (1 lb 2 oz) Chinese cabbage
1 tablespoon olive oil
250 g (9 oz/2¾ cups) bean sprouts
5 spring onions (scallions), cut into
    short pieces
2 garlic cloves, crushed
1 tablespoon olive oil
2 teaspoons sesame oil
2 tablespoons teriyaki marinade
½ teaspoon sugar
sweet chilli sauce, to taste

1   Cut the capsicum in half and remove the seeds and membrane. Cut into thin strips. Slice the mushrooms in half. Cut any large baby corn in half. Cut the cabbage into thick slices, then into squares.

2   Brush a hot barbecue grill plate or flat plate with oil. Put the capsicum, mushrooms, corn, cabbage, sprouts, spring onions and garlic onto the hotplate and cook for 4 minutes, tossing and stirring to prevent burning or sticking.

3   Mix together the olive oil, sesame oil, teriyaki marinade and sugar and pour over the vegetables. Stir thoroughly to coat and cook for 1 minute longer. Serve immediately, drizzled with sweet chilli sauce.

NOTE: *All the vegetables should be cut to about the same size to ensure even cooking.*

NUTRITION PER SERVE
Protein 5 g; Fat 8 g; Carbohydrate 8 g; Dietary
Fibre 8 g; Cholesterol 0 mg; 520 kJ (124 Cal)

Cut the capsicum into thin strips, the spring onions into lengths and the cabbage into squares.

Brush the barbecue hotplate with oil and then stir-fry the vegetables directly on the barbecue.

Pour the dressing over the stir-fried vegetables, toss and cook for a minute longer.

Herbed feta salad

PREPARATION TIME: 20 MINUTES + 30 MINUTES MARINATING | TOTAL COOKING TIME: 10 MINUTES | SERVES 8

2 slices thick white bread
200 g (7 oz) feta cheese
1 garlic clove, crushed
1 tablespoon chopped marjoram
1 tablespoon snipped chives
1 tablespoon chopped basil
2 tablespoons white wine vinegar
80 ml (2½ fl oz/⅓ cup) olive oil
1 red coral lettuce
1 green mignonette or oak leaf lettuce

1 Preheat the oven to 180°C (350°F/Gas 4). Remove the crusts from the bread and cut the bread into small cubes. Place on an oven tray in a single layer and bake for 10 minutes, until crisp and lightly golden. Transfer to a bowl and cool completely.

2 Cut the feta into small cubes and put in a bowl. Put the garlic, marjoram, chives, basil, vinegar and oil in a screw-top jar and shake well. Pour over the feta and cover with plastic wrap. Leave for at least 30 minutes, stirring occasionally.

3 Tear the lettuce into large pieces and put in a serving bowl. Add the feta with the dressing and bread cubes and toss the salad well.

NUTRITION PER SERVE
Protein 6 g; Fat 16 g; Carbohydrate 4 g; Dietary Fibre 1 g; Cholesterol 17 mg; 750 kJ (180 Cal)

Remove the crusts from the bread and then cut it into small cubes.

Cut the feta into cubes and then pour the dressing over and leave to marinate.

Add the bread cubes to the salad leaves and marinated feta.

Lentil salad

PREPARATION TIME: 15 MINUTES + 30 MINUTES STANDING | TOTAL COOKING TIME: 30 MINUTES | SERVES 4–6

½ onion

2 cloves

300 g (10½ oz/1½ cups) puy lentils

1 strip lemon zest

2 garlic cloves, peeled

1 fresh bay leaf

2 teaspoons ground cumin

2 tablespoons red wine vinegar

3 tablespoons olive oil

1 tablespoon lemon juice

2 tablespoons finely chopped mint

3 spring onions (scallions), finely chopped

1   Stud the onion with the cloves and place in a saucepan with the lentils, lemon zest, garlic, bay leaf, 1 teaspoon cumin and 875 ml (30 fl oz/ 3½ cups) water. Bring to the boil and cook over medium heat for 25–30 minutes, or until the water has been absorbed. Discard the onion, lemon zest and bay leaf. Reserve the garlic and finely chop.

2   Whisk together the vinegar, oil, lemon juice, garlic and remaining cumin. Stir through the lentils with the mint and spring onion. Season well. Leave for 30 minutes to let the flavours blend. Serve at room temperature.

NUTRITION PER SERVE (6)
Protein 13 g; Fat 11 g; Carbohydrate 20 g; Dietary Fibre 7.5 g; Cholesterol 0 mg; 930 kJ (222 Cal)

Stud the onion with the cloves and place in a saucepan with the lentils.

Cook the lentils, then discard the onion, lemon zest and bay leaf.

Whisk together the vinegar, oil, lemon juice, garlic and cumin.

Caramelised onion and potato salad

PREPARATION TIME: 20 MINUTES | TOTAL COOKING TIME: 1 HOUR | SERVES 10

2 tablespoons oil
6 red onions, thinly sliced
1 kg (2 lb 4 oz) small waxy
    potatoes, unpeeled
4 bacon slices, rind removed
30 g (1 oz/1 bunch) chives, snipped
250 g (9 oz/1 cup) mayonnaise
1 tablespoon dijon mustard
juice of 1 lemon
2 tablespoons sour cream

1   Heat the oil in a large heavy-based frying pan, add the onion and cook over low–medium heat for 40 minutes, or until very soft.

2   Cut the potatoes into large chunks (if they are small enough, leave them whole). Cook in boiling water for 10 minutes, or until just tender, then drain and cool slightly. (Do not overcook the potatoes or they will fall apart.)

3   Grill the bacon until crisp, drain on paper towels and cool slightly before coarsely chopping.

4   Put the potato, onion and chives in a large bowl, reserving a few chives for a garnish, and mix well.

5   Put the mayonnaise, mustard, lemon juice and sour cream in a bowl and whisk together. Pour over the salad and toss to coat. Sprinkle with the bacon and garnish with the reserved chives.

NOTE: *Kipfler (fingerling) potatoes are small and elongated. You can also use other waxy potatoes, such as pontiac or desirée, and cut them into pieces.*

NUTRITION PER SERVE
Protein 9 g; Fat 13 g; Carbohydrate 35 g; Dietary Fibre 4.5 g; Cholesterol 20 mg; 1221 kJ (292 Cal)

Cook the sliced onion over low–medium heat until soft and caramelised.

Wash the potatoes and cut them into large chunks, or leave whole if they are small enough.

Whisk together the mayonnaise, mustard, lemon juice and sour cream.

Warm marinated mushroom salad

PREPARATION TIME: 25 MINUTES + 20 MINUTES MARINATING | TOTAL COOKING TIME: 5 MINUTES | SERVES 4

750 g (1 lb 10 oz) mixed mushrooms
(such as baby button, oyster, Swiss brown,
shiitake and enoki)
2 garlic cloves, finely chopped
½ teaspoon green peppercorns, crushed
80 ml (2½ fl oz/⅓ cup) olive oil
80 ml (2½ fl oz/⅓ cup) orange juice
250 g (9 oz) salad leaves, watercress or baby
spinach leaves
1 teaspoon finely grated orange zest

1 Trim the mushroom stems and wipe the mushrooms with a damp paper towel. Cut any large mushrooms in half. Mix together the garlic, peppercorns, olive oil and orange juice. Pour over the mushrooms and marinate for about 20 minutes.

2 Arrange the salad leaves in a serving dish.

3 Drain the mushrooms, reserving the marinade. Cook the flat and button mushrooms on a hot, lightly oiled barbecue grill plate or flat plate for about 2 minutes. Add the softer mushrooms and cook for 1 minute, or until they just soften.

4 Scatter the mushrooms over the salad leaves and drizzle with the marinade. Sprinkle with orange zest and season well.

Trim the mushroom stems and wipe clean with paper towel. Cut any large mushrooms in half.

Mix together the garlic, peppercorns, olive oil and orange juice and pour over the mushrooms.

NUTRITION PER SERVE
Protein 10 g; Fat 15 g; Carbohydrate 5 g; Dietary
Fibre 5 g; Cholesterol 0 mg; 790 kJ (190 Cal)

Kipfler potato salad

PREPARATION TIME: 10 MINUTES | TOTAL COOKING TIME: 20–30 MINUTES | SERVES 6

1 kg (2 lb 4 oz) washed kipfler (fingerling)
   potatoes
125 g (4½ oz) bacon, chopped
oil, for frying
2 spring onions (scallions), chopped
125 g (4½ oz/½ cup) sour cream
2 tablespoons olive oil
2 tablespoons red wine vinegar
2 teaspoons dijon mustard
2 teaspoons wholegrain mustard

1 Boil the potatoes for 20 minutes, or until tender. Cut into thick slices on the diagonal.

2 Cook the bacon in a little oil until crispy and golden. Add to the potatoes and spring onion.

3 Whisk together the sour cream, olive oil, red wine vinegar and mustards. Pour the dressing over the potatoes and gently toss. Season with black pepper.

NUTRITION PER SERVE
Protein 7.8 g; Fat 18.4 g; Carbohydrate 23.2 g; Dietary Fibre 3.5 g; Cholesterol 38 mg; 1248 kJ (298 Cal)

Cook the chopped bacon in a little oil until crispy and golden.

Pour the dressing over the potatoes, bacon and spring onion.

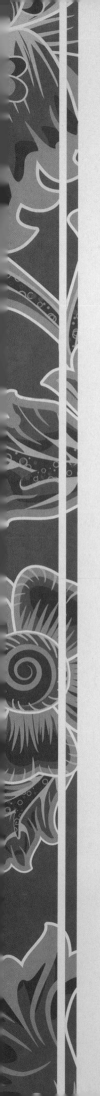

Desserts

Figs in honey syrup

PREPARATION TIME: 15 MINUTES | TOTAL COOKING TIME: 1 HOUR | SERVES 4

100 g (3½ oz) blanched whole almonds
12 whole fresh figs (see NOTE)
110 g (3¾ oz/½ cup) sugar
115 g (4 oz/⅓ cup) honey
2 tablespoons lemon juice
5 cm (2 inch) sliver lemon zest
1 cinnamon stick
250 g (9 oz/1 cup) Greek-style yoghurt

1 Preheat the oven to 180°C (350°F/Gas 4). Place the almonds on a baking tray and toast for 5 minutes, or until golden brown. Cool. Cut the tops off the figs and make a small crossways incision into the top of each one. Push an almond into the base of each fig. Roughly chop the remaining almonds.

2 Place 750 ml (26 fl oz/3 cups) water in a large saucepan, add the sugar and stir over medium heat until the sugar dissolves. Increase the heat and bring to the boil. Stir in the honey, lemon juice and zest and cinnamon stick. Reduce the heat, add the figs and cook for 30 minutes. Remove with a slotted spoon.

3 Boil the liquid over high heat for 15–20 minutes, or until thick and syrupy. Remove the cinnamon and zest. Cool the syrup slightly and pour over the figs. Sprinkle with the remaining almonds. Serve warm or cold with yoghurt.

NOTE: *You can also use 500 g (1 lb 2 oz) dried whole figs. Cover with 750 ml (26 fl oz/3 cups) cold water and soak for 8 hours. Drain, reserving the liquid. Push a blanched almond into the bottom of each fig. Place the liquid in a large saucepan, add the sugar and bring to the boil, stirring as the sugar dissolves. Add the honey, lemon juice, lemon zest and cinnamon stick, and continue the recipe as above.*

NUTRITION PER SERVE
Protein 11 g; Fat 17 g; Carbohydrate 74 g; Dietary Fibre 7 g; Cholesterol 10 mg; 2017 kJ (482 Cal)

Make a small crossways incision in the top of each fig.

Push a blanched almond into the base of each fig.

Using a slotted spoon, remove the figs from the pan of syrup.

Apple and pear sorbet

PREPARATION TIME: 10 MINUTES + FREEZING | TOTAL COOKING TIME: 10 MINUTES | SERVES 4–6

4 large green apples, peeled, cored
   and chopped
4 pears, peeled, cored and chopped
1 strip lemon zest
1 cinnamon stick
60 ml (2 fl oz/¼ cup) lemon juice
4 tablespoons caster (superfine) sugar
2 tablespoons Calvados or pear liqueur
   (optional)

1 Place the apple and pear in a large deep saucepan with the lemon zest, cinnamon stick and enough water to just cover the fruit. Cover and poach the fruit gently over medium–low heat for 6–8 minutes, or until tender. Remove the lemon zest and cinnamon stick. Place the fruit in a food processor and blend with the lemon juice until smooth.

2 Place the sugar in a saucepan with 80 ml (2½ fl oz/⅓ cup) water, bring to the boil and simmer for 1 minute. Add the fruit purée and the liqueur and combine well.

3 Pour into a shallow metal tray and freeze for 2 hours, or until the mixture is frozen around the edges. Transfer to a food processor or bowl and blend or beat until smooth. Pour back into the tray and return to the freezer. Repeat this process three times. For the final freezing, place in an airtight container—cover the surface with a piece of greaseproof paper and cover with a lid. Serve in small glasses or bowls.

Hint: Pour an extra nip of Calvados over the sorbet to serve.

Check if the fruit is tender by poking with the tip of a sharp knife.

Blend the partially frozen mixture in a food processor until smooth.

NUTRITION PER SERVE (6)
Fat 0.5 g; Protein 1 g; Carbohydrate 42 g; Dietary Fibre 4.5 g; Cholesterol 0 mg; 730 kJ (175 Cal)

Strawberries with balsamic vinegar

PREPARATION TIME: 10 MINUTES + 2 HOURS 30 MINUTES MARINATING | TOTAL COOKING TIME: NIL | SERVES 4

750 g (1 lb 10 oz) ripe strawberries
60 g (2¼ oz/¼ cup) caster (superfine) sugar
2 tablespoons balsamic vinegar
110 g (3¾ oz/½ cup) mascarpone cheese

1   Wipe the strawberries with a clean damp cloth and carefully remove the green stalks. If the strawberries are large, cut each one in half.

2   Place all the strawberries in a large glass bowl, sprinkle the caster sugar evenly over the top and toss gently to coat. Set aside for 2 hours to macerate, then sprinkle the balsamic vinegar over the strawberries. Toss them again, then refrigerate for about 30 minutes.

3   Spoon the strawberries into four glasses, drizzle with the syrup and top with a dollop of mascarpone.

NOTE: *If you leave the strawberries for more than 2 hours, it is best to refrigerate them.*

NUTRITION PER SERVE
Protein 6 g; Fat 11 g; Carbohydrate 20 g; Dietary Fibre 4 g; Cholesterol 30 mg; 830 kJ (200 Cal)

Hull the strawberries after wiping clean with a damp cloth.

Sprinkle the caster sugar evenly over the strawberries and toss to coat.

Use good-quality balsamic vinegar to sprinkle over the strawberries.

Peaches poached in wine

PREPARATION TIME: 20 MINUTES | TOTAL COOKING TIME: 20 MINUTES | SERVES 4

4 just-ripe yellow-fleshed slipstone peaches
    (see NOTE)
500 ml (17 fl oz/2 cups) sweet white wine,
    such as Sauternes
3 tablespoons orange liqueur
250 g (9 oz) sugar
1 cinnamon stick
1 vanilla bean, split
8 mint leaves
mascarpone cheese, to serve

1 Cut a small cross in the base of each peach. Immerse the peaches in boiling water for 30 seconds, then drain and cool slightly. Peel off the skin, cut in half and carefully remove the stones.

2 Place the wine, liqueur, sugar, cinnamon stick and vanilla bean in a deep-sided frying pan large enough to hold the peach halves in a single layer. Heat the mixture, stirring, until the sugar dissolves. Bring to the boil, then reduce the heat and simmer for 5 minutes. Add the peaches to the pan and simmer for 4 minutes, turning them over halfway through. Remove with a slotted spoon and leave to cool. Continue to simmer the syrup for 6–8 minutes, or until thick. Strain and set aside.

3 Arrange the peaches on a serving platter, cut side up. Spoon the syrup over the top and garnish each half with a mint leaf. Serve the peaches warm or chilled, with a dollop of mascarpone.

NOTE: *There are two types of peach, the slipstone and the clingstone. As the names imply, clingstone indicates that the flesh will cling to the stone, whereas the stones in slipstone or freestone peaches are easily removed without breaking up the flesh. Each has a variety with either yellow or white flesh, and all these peaches are equally delicious.*

NUTRITION PER SERVE
Protein 3 g; Fat 6.5 g; Carbohydrate 74 g; Dietary Fibre 2 g; Cholesterol 19 mg; 1900 kJ (455 Cal)

Peel the skin away from the cross cut in the base of the peaches.

Simmer the wine, liqueur, sugar, cinnamon and vanilla bean.

Lemon granita

PREPARATION TIME: 15 MINUTES + 2 HOURS FREEZING | TOTAL COOKING TIME: 5 MINUTES | SERVES 6

315 ml (10¾ fl oz/1¼ cups) lemon juice
1 tablespoon lemon zest
200 g (7 oz) caster (superfine) sugar

1 Place the lemon juice, lemon zest and caster sugar in a small saucepan and stir over low heat for 5 minutes, or until the sugar has dissolved. Remove from the heat and leave to cool.

2 Add 500 ml (17 fl oz/2 cups) water to the juice mixture and mix together well. Pour the mixture into a shallow 30 x 20 cm (12 x 8 inch) metal container and place in the freezer until the mixture is beginning to freeze around the edges. Scrape the frozen sections back into the mixture with a fork. Repeat every 30 minutes until the mixture has even-sized ice crystals. Beat the mixture with a fork just before serving. To serve, spoon the lemon granita into six chilled glasses.

NUTRITION PER SERVE
Protein 0 g; Fat 0 g; Carbohydrate 35 g; Dietary Fibre 0 g; Cholesterol 0 mg; 592 kJ (140 Cal)

Stir the juice, zest and sugar over low heat until the sugar has dissolved.

Scrape the frozen edges of the mixture back into the centre.

Beat the granita mixture with a fork just prior to serving to break up the crystals.

Berries in Champagne jelly

PREPARATION TIME: 10 MINUTES + OVERNIGHT REFRIGERATION | TOTAL COOKING TIME: 5 MINUTES | SERVES 8

1 litre (35 fl oz/4 cups) Champagne or
    sparkling white wine
1½ tablespoons gelatine
250 g (9 oz) sugar
4 strips lemon zest
4 strips orange zest
250 g (9 oz) small hulled and
    halved strawberries
250 g (9 oz) blueberries

1   Pour 500 ml (17 fl oz/2 cups) Champagne into a bowl and let the bubbles subside. Sprinkle the gelatine over the Champagne in an even layer. Leave until the gelatine is spongy—do not stir. Place the remaining Champagne in a large saucepan with the sugar, lemon and orange zest, and heat gently, until all the sugar has dissolved.

2   Remove the saucepan from the heat, add the gelatine mixture and stir until thoroughly dissolved. Leave the jelly to cool completely, then remove the lemon and orange zest.

3   Divide the berries among eight 125 ml (4 fl oz/½ cup) glasses and gently pour the jelly over the top. Refrigerate for 6 hours or overnight, or until fully set. Remove from the fridge 15 minutes before serving.

NUTRITION PER SERVE
Protein 3 g; Fat 0 g; Carbohydrate 37 g; Dietary Fibre 1 g; Cholesterol 0 mg; 965 kJ (230 Cal)

Sprinkle the gelatine over the Champagne and then leave to go spongy.

Leave the jelly to cool completely before removing the lemon and orange zest.

Put the berries in the glasses and then pour jelly over the top.

Baked cheesecake

PREPARATION TIME: 30 MINUTES + 20 MINUTES REFRIGERATION | TOTAL COOKING TIME: 55 MINUTES | SERVES 8

250 g (9 oz) butternut cookies
1 teaspoon mixed (pumpkin pie) spice
100 g (3½ oz) butter, melted
500 g (1 lb 2 oz) cream cheese, softened
170 g (6 oz/¾ cup) caster (superfine) sugar
4 eggs
1 teaspoon vanilla essence
1 tablespoon orange juice
1 tablespoon finely grated orange zest

TOPPING
250 g (9 oz/1 cup) sour cream
½ teaspoon vanilla essence
3 teaspoons orange juice
1 tablespoon caster (superfine) sugar
freshly grated nutmeg

1 Lightly grease the base of a 20 cm (8 inch) spring-form cake tin. Finely crush the biscuits in a food processor for 30 seconds, or put them in a plastic bag and roll with a rolling pin. Transfer to a bowl and add the mixed spice and butter. Stir until all the crumbs are moistened, then spoon into the tin and press firmly into the base and side. Chill for 20 minutes, or until firm.

2 Preheat the oven to 180°C (350°F/Gas 4). Beat the cream cheese until smooth. Add the sugar and beat until smooth. Add the eggs, one at a time, beating well after each addition. Mix in the vanilla, orange juice and zest.

3 Pour the mixture into the crumb case and bake for 45 minutes, or until just firm. To make the topping, combine the sour cream, vanilla, orange juice and sugar in a bowl. Spread over the hot cheesecake, sprinkle with nutmeg and return to the oven for 7 minutes. Cool, then refrigerate until firm.

NUTRITION PER SERVE
Protein 10 g; Fat 50 g; Carbohydrate 45 g; Dietary Fibre 0.5 g; Cholesterol 230 mg; 2885 kJ (690 Cal)

Press the biscuit mixture into a spring-form cake tin with the back of a spoon.

Add the eggs one at a time to the cream cheese mixture and beat well.

When the filling is smooth, mix in the vanilla, orange juice and zest.

Grilled oranges with caramel mint butter

PREPARATION TIME: 20 MINUTES I TOTAL COOKING TIME: 20 MINUTES I SERVES 4

6 oranges
75 g (2½ oz/⅓ cup) sugar
3 tablespoons pouring (whipping) cream
45 g (1½ oz) unsalted butter, chopped
2 teaspoons grated orange zest
2 tablespoons finely chopped mint

1 Peel the oranges in a circular motion, cutting only deeply enough to remove all the white membrane. Cut the oranges into thin slices.

2 Place the sugar and 3 tablespoons water in a small saucepan. Cook over very low heat without boiling until the sugar has dissolved (shake occasionally but do not stir). Increase the heat and bring the syrup to the boil. Cook until deep golden. Remove from the heat and gradually add the cream (the mixture will become lumpy) (be careful when adding the cream as the hot mixture may splatter). Return to the heat and stir until the cream dissolves.

3 Add the butter, orange zest and mint to the saucepan and whisk until blended. Transfer to a bowl and chill until firm.

4 Preheat the grill. Arrange the orange slices slightly overlapping in a 23 cm (9 inch) round shallow ovenproof dish. Dot with the caramel butter and grill until the butter has melted and the oranges are hot.

Add the butter, orange zest and mint to the pan and whisk to blend.

Arrange the orange slices in an ovenproof dish and dot with the caramel butter.

NUTRITION PER SERVE
Protein 2 g; Fat 16 g; Carbohydrate 36 g; Dietary Fibre 4 g; Cholesterol 49 mg; 1215 kJ (290 Cal)

Coconut lime ice cream

PREPARATION TIME: 10 MINUTES + 30 MINUTES FREEZING | TOTAL COOKING TIME: NIL | SERVES 4

30 g (1 oz/⅓ cup) desiccated coconut
1½ tablespoons grated lime zest
80 ml (2½ fl oz/⅓ cup) lime juice
4 tablespoons coconut milk powder
1 litre (35 fl oz/4 cups) good-quality vanilla ice
 cream, softened
coconut macaroon biscuits, to serve

1 Put the coconut, lime zest, lime juice
and coconut milk powder in a bowl and mix
together well.

2 Add to the ice cream and fold through with
a large metal spoon until evenly incorporated.
Work quickly so that the ice cream does not
melt. Return the ice cream to the freezer and
freeze for 30 minutes to firm. Serve in glasses
with coconut macaroons.

Mix together the desiccated coconut, lime zest, lime juice and coconut milk powder.

Add the coconut mixture to the ice cream and fold in with a large metal spoon.

NUTRITION PER SERVE
Protein 5 g; Fat 19.5 g; Carbohydrate 19 g; Dietary
Fibre 1.5 g; Cholesterol 30 mg; 1230 kJ (293 Cal)

Spiced apple slice

PREPARATION TIME: 25 MINUTES + 30 MINUTES REFRIGERATION | TOTAL COOKING TIME: 55 MINUTES | SERVES 8

750 g (1 lb 10 oz) green apples
75 g (2½ oz/⅓ cup) sugar
½ teaspoon ground cloves
2 tablespoons lemon juice
125 g (4½ oz/1 cup) plain (all-purpose) flour
125 g (4½ oz/1 cup) self-raising flour
1 teaspoon ground cloves, extra
½ teaspoon ground cinnamon
150 g (5½ oz) butter
125 g (4½ oz/½ cup) caster (superfine) sugar
1 teaspoon vanilla essence
1 egg, lightly beaten
1 tablespoon milk, or as needed
1 tablespoon caster (superfine) sugar, extra
1 teaspoon ground cinnamon, extra

NUTRITION PER SERVE
Protein 5 g; Fat 17 g; Carbohydrate 64 g; Dietary
Fibre 3 g; Cholesterol 72 mg; 1772 kJ (423 Cal)

1 Brush a 20 x 30 cm (8 x 12 inch) shallow tin with oil. Line the base with baking paper and grease the paper. Preheat the oven to 180°C (350°F/Gas 4). Peel, core and slice the apples and put in a saucepan with the sugar, cloves and lemon juice. Stir over low heat to warm. Cover and simmer, stirring often, for 20 minutes, or until soft. Remove from the heat, drain and cool.

2 Sift the flours with the extra cloves and the ½ teaspoon cinnamon. Beat the butter and sugar until light and creamy. Add the vanilla and egg and beat thoroughly. Fold in the flour in batches. If the mixture is too dry, add a little milk. Knead gently on a lightly floured surface until smooth. Divide in half, cover with plastic wrap and chill for 30 minutes.

3 Roll out one portion of pastry to fit the base of the tin. Spread with apple filling. Place the second pastry sheet on top of the filling and press down gently.

4 Brush the top with milk and sprinkle with the extra sugar and cinnamon. Bake for 30 minutes, or until golden brown. Leave for 15 minutes, then turn onto a wire rack to cool.

Peel, core and slice the apples and put in a saucepan with the sugar, cloves and lemon juice.

Line the tray with one of the pastry sheets and spread the filling on top.

Brush the top of the slice with milk and then sprinkle with sugar and cinnamon.

Mandarin ice

PREPARATION TIME: 10 MINUTES + FREEZING | TOTAL COOKING TIME: 10 MINUTES | SERVES 4–6

10 mandarins
125 g (4½ oz/½ cup) caster (superfine) sugar

1   Squeeze the mandarins to make 500 ml (17 fl oz/2 cups) juice.

2   Place the sugar and 250 ml (9 fl oz/1 cup) water in a small saucepan. Stir over low heat until the sugar has dissolved, then simmer for 5 minutes. Remove from the heat and leave to cool slightly.

3   Stir the mandarin juice into the sugar syrup, then pour into a shallow metal tray. Freeze for 2 hours, or until frozen. Transfer to a food processor and blend until slushy. Return to the freezer and repeat the process three more times.

NUTRITION PER SERVE (6)
Fat 0 g; Protein 0.5 g; Carbohydrate 5 g; Dietary Fibre 0 g; Cholesterol 0 mg; 105 kJ (25 Cal)

Squeeze the mandarins (as you would other citrus fruits) to give 2 cups of juice.

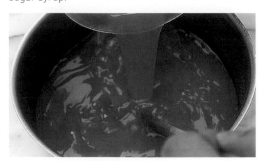

Stir the mandarin juice into the saucepan of sugar syrup.

Blend the frozen mixture in a food processor until it is slushy.

Pavlova

PREPARATION TIME: 15 MINUTES | TOTAL COOKING TIME: 40 MINUTES | SERVES 8

6 egg whites
375 g (13 oz/1½ cups) caster (superfine) sugar
250 ml (9 fl oz/1 cup) cream, whipped
125 g (4½ oz) strawberries, halved
2 kiwi fruit, peeled and sliced
1 banana, sliced
pulp of 2 passionfruit

1   Preheat the oven to 150°C (300°F/Gas 2). Line a baking tray with baking paper and mark with a 23 cm (9 inch) circle. Beat the egg whites until soft peaks form. Gradually beat in the sugar, then beat for several minutes, or until thick and glossy.

2   Spoon the meringue mixture onto the circle on the tray. Smooth the edge and top with a flat-bladed knife.

3   Bake for 40 minutes, or until pale and crisp. Turn off the oven and leave the meringue inside to cool, with the door ajar. Just before serving, spread with cream and top with strawberries, kiwi fruit, banana and passionfruit pulp.

STORAGE: *Pavlova shell can be made 1 day in advance and stored in an airtight container. Top with cream and fruit just before serving.*

NUTRITION PER SERVE
Protein 3 g; Fat 14 g; Carbohydrate 52 g; Dietary Fibre 1 g; Cholesterol 40 mg; 901 kJ (215 Cal)

Beat the egg whites to soft peaks, then gradually beat in the sugar.

Spread the meringue onto the paper-lined tray, using the circle as a guide.

Just before serving, spread the cooled meringue with the whipped cream.

Tiramisu

PREPARATION TIME: 30 MINUTES + AT LEAST 2 HOURS REFRIGERATION | TOTAL COOKING TIME: NIL | SERVES 6

750 ml (26 fl oz/3 cups) strong black
    coffee, cooled
3 tablespoons Marsala or
    coffee-flavoured liqueur
2 eggs, separated
3 tablespoons caster (superfine) sugar
250 g (9 oz) mascarpone cheese
250 ml (9 fl oz/1 cup) cream, whipped
16 large savoiardi (lady fingers)
2 tablespoons dark cocoa powder

1 Mix together the coffee and Marsala in a bowl and set aside. Using electric beaters, beat the egg yolks and sugar in a bowl for 3 minutes, or until thick and pale. Add the mascarpone cheese and mix until just combined. Transfer to a large bowl and fold in the cream.

2 Beat the egg whites until soft peaks form. Fold quickly and lightly into the cream mixture.

3 Dip half the biscuits into the coffee mixture, then drain off any excess coffee and arrange in the base of a 2.5 litre (87 fl oz/10 cup) ceramic dish. Spread half the cream mixture over the biscuits.

4 Dip the remaining biscuits into the remaining coffee mixture and repeat the layers. Smooth the surface and dust liberally with the cocoa powder. Refrigerate for at least 2 hours, or until firm.

STORAGE: *Tiramisu is best made a day in advance to let the flavours develop. Refrigerate until ready to serve.*

NUTRITION PER SERVE
Protein 7.5 g; Fat 24 g; Carbohydrate 28 g; Dietary Fibre 1 g; Cholesterol 180 mg; 1545 kJ (370 Cal)

Add the mascarpone cheese to the egg yolks and sugar and mix until just combined.

Fold the beaten egg whites gently into the cream mixture with a metal spoon.

Dip half the lady fingers in the coffee mixture, drain, and arrange in the serving dish.

Red fruit salad with berries

PREPARATION TIME: 5 MINUTES + 2 HOURS COOLING AND REFRIGERATION | TOTAL COOKING TIME: 5 MINUTES | SERVES 6

SYRUP
60 g (2¼ oz/¼ cup) caster (superfine) sugar
125 ml (4 fl oz/½ cup) dry red wine
1 star anise
1 teaspoon finely chopped lemon zest

250 g (9 oz) strawberries, hulled and halved
150 g (5½ oz) blueberries
150 g (5½ oz) raspberries, mulberries or other
   red berries
250 g (9 oz) cherries
5 small red plums (about 250 g/9 oz), stones
   removed, quartered
low-fat yoghurt, to serve

1   To make the syrup, place the sugar, wine, star anise, lemon zest and 125 ml (4 fl oz/½ cup) water in a small saucepan. Bring to the boil over medium heat, stirring to dissolve the sugar. Boil the syrup for 3 minutes, then set aside to cool for 30 minutes. When cool, strain the syrup.

2   Mix the fruit together in a large bowl and pour on the red wine syrup. Mix well to coat the fruit in the syrup and refrigerate for 1 hour 30 minutes. Serve the fruit dressed with a little syrup and the yoghurt.

Remove the stems, then cut the strawberries in half.

Mix together the strawberries, blueberries, raspberries, cherries and plums.

NUTRITION PER SERVE
Fat 0 g; Protein 2 g; Carbohydrate 24 g; Dietary
Fibre 5 g; Cholesterol 0 mg; 500 kJ (120 Cal)

Ginger and lychee jelly

PREPARATION TIME: 10 MINUTES + 4 HOURS SETTING | TOTAL COOKING TIME: 5 MINUTES | SERVES 6

500 g (1 lb 2 oz) tin lychees
500 ml (17 fl oz/2 cups) clear, unsweetened
    apple juice
80 ml (2½ fl oz/⅓ cup) strained lime juice
2 tablespoons caster (superfine) sugar
3 x 3 cm (1¼ x 1¼ inch) piece fresh ginger,
    peeled and thinly sliced
4 sheets gelatine
mint, to garnish

1 Drain the syrup from the lychees and reserve 250 ml (9 fl oz/1 cup) of the syrup. Place the reserved syrup, apple juice, lime juice, sugar and ginger in a saucepan. Bring to the boil, then simmer for 5 minutes. Strain into a heatproof bowl.

2 Place the gelatine sheets in a large bowl of cold water and soak for 2 minutes, or until they soften. Squeeze out the excess water, then add to the syrup. Stir until dissolved. Leave to cool.

3 Pour 2 tablespoons of jelly into each of six 150 ml (5 fl oz) wine glasses, and divide the lychees among them. Refrigerate for 3 hours, or until the jelly has set. Spoon the remaining jelly over the fruit and refrigerate for 2–3 hours, or until set. Garnish with mint leaves.

NUTRITION PER SERVE
Fat 0 g; Protein 1 g; Carbohydrate 31 g; Dietary
Fibre 0.5 g; Cholesterol 0 mg; 530 kJ (125 Cal)

After soaking, squeeze the sheets of gelatine to remove any excess water.

Stir the gelatine sheets into the hot liquid until they have dissolved.

Divide the lychees among the wine glasses, gently dropping them into the jelly.

Creamy lime tart

PREPARATION TIME: 30 MINUTES + 20 MINUTES REFRIGERATION | TOTAL COOKING TIME: 1 HOUR | SERVES 12

155 g (5½ oz/1¼ cups) plain
   (all-purpose) flour
95 g (3¼ oz/1 cup) ground almonds
90 g (3¼ oz) butter, chopped

FILLING
6 egg yolks
115 g (4 oz/½ cup) caster (superfine) sugar
100 g (3½ oz) butter, melted
80 ml (2½ fl oz/⅓ cup) lime juice
2 teaspoons finely grated lime zest
2 teaspoons gelatine
125 ml (4 fl oz/½ cup) cream, whipped
110 g (3¾ oz/½ cup) sugar
finely shredded zest of 4 limes

1 Preheat the oven to 180°C (350°F/Gas 4). Sift the flour into a large bowl and add the almonds and butter. Rub in the butter until the mixture is fine and crumbly. Add 1–2 tablespoons cold water and mix to a firm dough, adding more water if necessary. Turn out onto a lightly floured surface and roll out to fit a 23 cm (9 inch) fluted flan (tart) tin. Trim the edge and refrigerate for 20 minutes.

2 Line with baking paper and beads or dried beans or rice and bake for 15 minutes. Remove the paper and beads and bake the pastry shell for a further 10 minutes, or until lightly golden. Cool completely.

3 To make the filling, put the egg yolks, sugar, butter, lime juice and zest in a heatproof bowl. Whisk together to dissolve the sugar. Place the bowl over a pan of simmering water and stir constantly for 15 minutes, or until thickened. Leave to cool slightly.

4 Put the gelatine and 1 tablespoon water in a small bowl. Leave until spongy, then stir until dissolved. Stir into the lime curd. Cool to room temperature, stirring occasionally.

5 Fold the cream through the lime curd and pour into the pastry case. Refrigerate for 2–3 hours, or until set, removing 15 minutes before serving. Put the sugar in a small saucepan with 3 tablespoons water. Stir without boiling until the sugar has completely dissolved. Bring to the boil, add the lime zest and simmer for 3 minutes. Remove the zest and dry on a rack then use to decorate the tart.

NUTRITION PER SERVE
Protein 4 g; Fat 21 g; Carbohydrate 32 g; Dietary Fibre 1 g; Cholesterol 144 mg; 1391 kJ (332 Cal)

Blind bake the pastry case, filled with baking paper and baking beads or dried beans.

Mix the gelatine with the water and then stir into the lime curd.

To make the glazed lime zest, simmer the zest for 3 minutes in sugar syrup, then drain on a rack.

Chocolate mint ice cream

PREPARATION TIME: 25 MINUTES + FREEZING | TOTAL COOKING TIME: 10 MINUTES | SERVES 6

250 ml (9 fl oz/1 cup) pouring
  (whipping) cream
3 tablespoons chopped mint
100 g (3½ oz) dark chocolate, broken
60 g (2¼ oz) milk chocolate, broken
2 eggs, lightly beaten
1 tablespoon caster (superfine) sugar

1   Place the cream and mint in a small saucepan. Stir over low heat until the cream is almost boiling. Cool slightly. Add the chocolate to the cream. Stir over low heat until the chocolate has melted and the mixture is smooth.

2   Whisk the eggs and sugar in a small bowl until creamy. Gradually add the warm chocolate mixture through a strainer. Discard the mint. Whisk until well combined and then cool.

3   Freeze the mixture in an ice-cream machine according to the manufacturer's instructions. Alternatively, freeze in a metal container until just firm around the edges. Remove from the freezer and beat for 1 minute. Return to the freezer and freeze overnight.

STORAGE: *Ice cream can be stored in the freezer for up to 3 weeks.*

NUTRITION PER SERVE
Protein 5 g; Fat 27 g; Carbohydrate 21 g; Dietary Fibre 0 g; Cholesterol 118 mg; 1413 kJ (338 Cal)

Bring the cream to boiling point then allow to cool a little and add the chocolate.

Add the warm chocolate mixture slowly, through a strainer, discarding the mint.

If you don't have an ice-cream machine, freeze the mixture and then beat.

Strawberry trifle

PREPARATION TIME: 20 MINUTES + 4 HOURS REFRIGERATION | TOTAL COOKING TIME: NIL | SERVES 8

2 x 85 g (3 oz) packets red jelly crystals
250 ml (9 fl oz/1 cup) brandy or rum
250 ml (9 fl oz/1 cup) milk
2 x 250 g (9 oz) packets thin savoiardi
    (lady fingers)
500 g (1 lb 2 oz) strawberries, sliced
750 ml (26 fl oz/3 cups) custard
315 ml (10¾ fl oz/1¼ cups) cream, whipped

1 Mix the jelly crystals with 440 ml
(15¼ fl oz/1¾ cups) boiling water and stir to
dissolve. Pour into a shallow tin and refrigerate
until the jelly has just set but is not firm.

2 Combine the brandy and milk in a dish.
Dip half the biscuits in the brandy mixture then
place in a single layer in a 3 litre (105 fl oz/
12 cup) glass or ceramic dish. Spoon half the
jelly over the biscuits. Scatter with half the
strawberries and then half of the custard.

3 Dip the remaining lady fingers in the brandy
mixture and place evenly over the custard,
followed by the remaining jelly and custard.
Spread the whipped cream evenly over the
custard and top with the remaining strawberries.
Cover and refrigerate for 4 hours before serving.

NUTRITION PER SERVE
Protein 13 g; Fat 24 g; Carbohydrate 75 g; Dietary
Fibre 2 g; Cholesterol 165 mg; 2570 kJ (615 Cal)

Using a small sharp knife, hull the strawberries and cut into slices.

Spoon half the jelly over the biscuits before scattering on half the strawberries.

Dip the remaining biscuits in the brandy mixture and layer evenly over the custard.

Ginger pear cheesecake

PREPARATION TIME: 25 MINUTES + 3 HOURS REFRIGERATION | TOTAL COOKING TIME: NIL | SERVES 8

250 g (9 oz) gingernut biscuits (ginger snaps)
2 tablespoons caster (superfine) sugar
125 g (4½ oz) butter, melted

FILLING
1 tablespoon gelatine
375 g (13 oz) cream cheese
80 g (2¾ oz/⅓ cup) caster (superfine) sugar
1 tablespoon lemon juice
250 ml (9 fl oz/1 cup) cream, whipped
425 g (15 oz) tin pear halves, drained
   and sliced
2 tablespoons chopped glacé
   (candied) ginger

1 Brush a 20 cm (8 inch) spring-form cake tin with melted butter or oil. Chop the biscuits to crumbs in a food processor. Transfer to a bowl, add the sugar and butter and mix well. Press firmly into the tin and refrigerate for 20 minutes.

2 To make the filling, put the gelatine in a small bowl with 3 tablespoons water. Leave until spongy, then stir until dissolved. Beat the cream cheese until softened. Add the caster sugar and beat for 3 minutes. Add the lemon juice and beat until combined. Add a little of this mixture to the gelatine and mix well, then add all the gelatine to the filling mixture. Fold in the whipped cream.

3 Arrange a layer of pear slices on the biscuit crust, then pour over half the filling. Top with another layer of pears and the remaining filling. Refrigerate for 3 hours or until set. Decorate with chopped glacé ginger.

NUTRITION PER SERVE
Protein 6 g; Fat 42 g; Carbohydrate 43 g; Dietary Fibre 1 g; Cholesterol 128 mg; 2372 kJ (567 Cal)

Chop the biscuits to crumbs in a food processor (or put in a plastic bag and crush with a rolling pin).

Beat the cream cheese and sugar together and then add the lemon juice.

Arrange layers of pear slices and then add the cream cheese filling.

Fruit kebabs with cardamom syrup

PREPARATION TIME: 15 MINUTES + 1 HOUR MARINATING | TOTAL COOKING TIME: 5 MINUTES | MAKES 8 KEBABS

¼ small pineapple, peeled
1 peach
1 banana, peeled
16 strawberries

CARDAMOM SYRUP
2 tablespoons honey
30 g (1 oz) butter, melted
½ teaspoon ground cardamom
1 tablespoon rum or brandy
1 tablespoon soft brown sugar

1 Cut the pineapple into bite-sized pieces. Cut the peach into 8 wedges and slice the banana. Thread all the fruit pieces alternately onto skewers and place in a shallow dish.

2 To make the cardamom syrup, mix together the honey, butter, cardamom, rum and sugar and pour over the kebabs, brushing to coat. Cover and leave the kebabs at room temperature for 1 hour.

3 Cook the kebabs on a hot, lightly oiled barbecue grill plate or flat plate for 5 minutes. Brush with the syrup during cooking. Serve drizzled with the remaining syrup, topped with ice cream.

NUTRITION PER KEBAB
Protein 1 g; Fat 2 g; Carbohydrate 16 g; Dietary Fibre 2 g; Cholesterol 6 mg; 376 kJ (90 Cal)

Cut the fruit into bite-sized pieces and thread onto the skewers.

Mix together the honey, butter, cardamom, rum and sugar to make the syrup.

Cook the kebabs on a hot barbecue, brushing with the syrup during cooking.

Poached apples with cloves, mint and basil

PREPARATION TIME: 15 MINUTES | TOTAL COOKING TIME: 30 MINUTES | SERVES 4

4 large or 6 small green apples
2 tablespoons lemon juice
110 g (3¾ oz/½ cup) sugar
4 whole cloves
4 mint sprigs
6 basil leaves

1 Peel and core the apples and cut into quarters. Put the lemon juice, sugar, cloves and mint in a saucepan with 625 ml (21½ fl oz/ 2½ cups) water. Stir over low heat without boiling until the sugar dissolves. Bring to the boil.

2 Add the apple to the saucepan. Cook over low heat, partially covered, for 10 minutes or until the apple is soft but not breaking up. Add the basil. Remove from the heat and set aside until cold.

3 Carefully remove the apple segments from the syrup and place in a bowl. Pour the syrup through a sieve onto the apple. Serve chilled with cream or yoghurt.

STORAGE: *Store for up to 4 days in an airtight container in the fridge.*

NUTRITION PER SERVE
Protein 0.5 g; Fat 0 g; Carbohydrate 51 g; Dietary Fibre 3 g; Cholesterol 0 mg; 834 kJ (199 Cal)

Peel and core the apples and then cut each apple into quarters.

Bring the lemon juice, sugar, cloves, mint and water to the boil and add the apple.

Put the apple in a bowl and then pour the syrup over the top through a sieve.

Chocolate mousse flan

PREPARATION TIME: 35 MINUTES | TOTAL COOKING TIME: 5 MINUTES | SERVES 10

250 g (9 oz) plain chocolate biscuits, finely crushed
125 g (4½ oz) butter, melted

FILLING
200 g (7 oz) dark cooking chocolate, chopped
2 tablespoons pouring (whipping) cream
2 egg yolks
2 teaspoons gelatine
170 ml (5½ fl oz/⅔ cup) cream, whipped, extra
2 egg whites

TOPPING
1½ teaspoons instant coffee
250 ml (9 fl oz/1 cup) pouring (whipping) cream
1 tablespoon caster (superfine) sugar
cocoa powder, for dusting

1 Brush a 28 cm (11¼ inch) round fluted flan (tart) tin with melted butter or oil. Line the base with paper. Mix the biscuit crumbs and butter and press into the tin. Refrigerate until firm.

2 To make the filling, put the chocolate and cream in a small saucepan. Stir over low heat until smooth. Cool slightly, then stir in the egg yolks. Sprinkle the gelatine over 1 tablespoon water in a small bowl and leave until spongy, then stir. Cool slightly and stir into the filling. Fold in the whipped cream.

3 Beat the egg whites until soft peaks form. Fold into the filling and spread over the biscuit base. Refrigerate until set. Just before serving, remove from the tin and spread with the topping.

4 To make the topping, dissolve the coffee in 3 teaspoons water. Stir in the cream and sugar. Beat until soft peaks form, then spread over the flan. Dust with sifted cocoa powder to serve.

NUTRITION PER SERVE
Protein 6 g; Fat 37 g; Carbohydrate 32 g; Dietary Fibre 1 g; Cholesterol 158 mg; 1983 kJ (474 Cal)

Mix together the biscuit crumbs and melted butter and press into the tin.

Beat the egg whites until soft peaks form and then fold into the filling.

Just before you are ready to serve, spread the topping over the flan.

Basics—marinades and more

Sauces and dips for meatballs

Meatballs

MAKES 45 MEATBALLS

Combine 750 g (1 lb 10 oz) lean minced (ground) beef, 1 very finely chopped onion, 1 lightly beaten egg, 2 crushed garlic cloves, 2–3 tablespoons fresh breadcrumbs and lots of salt and freshly ground black pepper in a large bowl. Use your hands to mix well. Then wet your hands and roll tablespoons of the minced beef mixture into balls. You can thread the meatballs onto wooden skewers that have been soaked in cold water for 30 minutes to prevent scorching. Cook on a hot, lightly oiled barbecue grill plate or flat plate for about 10 minutes, or until the meat is cooked through. Serve the meatballs with two or three of the following sauces.

Barbecue sauce

MAKES ENOUGH FOR 15 MEATBALLS

Finely chop 1 small onion. Put a little oil in a frying pan and add the onion. Cook over low heat for 3 minutes, or until the onion is soft but not browned. Add 1 tablespoon each of malt vinegar, worcestershire sauce and soft brown sugar, plus 80 ml (2½ fl oz/⅓ cup) tomato sauce (ketchup). Bring the mixture to the boil and then reduce the heat and simmer for about 3 minutes, or until the sauce has slightly thickened. Serve the barbecue sauce warm or at room temperature with the meatballs.

Capsicum mayonnaise

MAKES ENOUGH FOR 15 MEATBALLS

Cut a large red capsicum (pepper) in half, remove the seeds and membrane and brush the skin lightly with oil. Grill, skin side up, until the skin blisters and blackens. Cover the capsicum with a tea towel (dish towel) or put in a paper or plastic bag to cool. When cool enough to handle, peel away the skin and place the flesh in a food processor. Add 185 g (6½ oz/¾ cup) whole egg mayonnaise, 1–2 garlic cloves, salt, pepper and a squeeze of lemon juice. Process until smooth. You could also add some chopped basil.

Chilli and lime sauce

MAKES ENOUGH FOR 15 MEATBALLS

Combine 60 ml (2 fl oz/¼ cup) sweet chilli sauce, 2 teaspoons soft brown sugar, 1 teaspoon finely grated lime zest, 3–4 teaspoons lime juice and 1 tablespoon freshly chopped basil.

Coriander sauce

MAKES ENOUGH FOR 15 MEATBALLS

In a bowl, combine 60 ml (2 fl oz/¼ cup) fish sauce, 1 tablespoon white vinegar, 2–3 teaspoons finely chopped fresh red chillies, 1 teaspoon sugar and 3 teaspoons chopped coriander (cilantro). Add a good squeeze of lime juice, mix well and serve.

Dill sauce

MAKES ENOUGH FOR 15 MEATBALLS

Combine 125 g (4½ oz/½ cup) each of plain yoghurt and sour cream, 1 tablespoon horseradish cream, 4 tablespoons chopped dill, 2 finely chopped spring onions (scallions) and salt and pepper. Mix well and serve chilled.

Herb sauce

MAKES ENOUGH FOR 15 MEATBALLS

Mix together 200 g (7 oz) plain yoghurt, 1 tablespoon each of chopped mint, coriander (cilantro) and lemon thyme, 2 tablespoons pouring (whipping) cream and 1 teaspoon freshly grated ginger. You could also add 1 small peeled, seeded and finely chopped Lebanese (short) cucumber.

Peanut sauce

MAKES ENOUGH FOR 15 MEATBALLS

Heat 3 teaspoons peanut oil in a pan. Add 1 small finely chopped onion and cook for 3 minutes, or until soft. Stir in 2 crushed garlic cloves, 2 teaspoons each of grated fresh ginger and ground cumin and 1 teaspoon red curry paste. Cook, stirring, for 1 minute. Stir in 375 ml (13 fl oz/1½ cups) coconut milk, 80 g (2¾ oz/½ cup) very finely chopped peanuts and 2 tablespoons soft brown sugar. Simmer over low heat for 5 minutes, or until slightly thickened. Add a little lemon juice. Serve the sauce warm.

Marinades and butters for meat

Asian marinade

MAKES 250 ML (9 FL OZ/1 CUP)

Mix together 2 crushed garlic cloves, 3 tablespoons each of soy sauce, sweet chilli sauce and teriyaki marinade, 1 tablespoon lemon juice and 1 teaspoon each of sesame oil and peanut oil. Place in a shallow, non-metallic dish, add 1 kg (2 lb 4 oz) meat and toss well to coat. Marinate in the fridge overnight before cooking on the barbecue.

Cajun spice marinade

MAKES 170 ML (5½ FL OZ/⅔ CUP)

Combine 80 ml (2½ fl oz/⅓ cup) olive oil, 2 tablespoons each of freshly ground black pepper, sweet paprika and white pepper into a bowl, add 1 tablespoon each of onion powder and garlic powder, 2 teaspoons dried oregano leaves and 1 teaspoon each of dried thyme leaves and cayenne pepper. Place in a shallow dish, add 1 kg (2 lb 4 oz) meat and toss well to coat. Marinate in the fridge for at least 3 hours before cooking on the barbecue.

Indian spice marinade

MAKES 250 ML (9 FL OZ/1 CUP)

Combine 250 g (9 oz/1 cup) yoghurt, 1 tablespoon each of grated onion and ginger, 2 crushed garlic cloves and 1 teaspoon each of brown sugar, ground turmeric, ground cumin, ground chilli and ground coriander. Place in a shallow, non-metallic dish, add 1 kg (2 lb 4 oz) meat and toss well to coat. Marinate in the fridge overnight before cooking on the barbecue.

Orange butter

SERVES 6

Beat 125 g (4½ oz/½ cup) butter until light and creamy, add 1 tablespoon chopped mint and 1 teaspoon each of orange marmalade and dijon mustard and mix until smooth. Roll the butter out between 2 pieces of baking paper and refrigerate until firm. Using small cookie cutters, cut out shapes from the butter and chill until ready to use. Delicious with 1 kg (2 lb 4 oz) barbecued lamb or beef.

Rosemary mustard butter

SERVES 6

Beat 125 g (4½ oz/½ cup) butter until light and creamy, add 3 tablespoons wholegrain mustard, 1 tablespoon chopped rosemary and 1 teaspoon each of lemon juice, lemon zest and honey. Mix together until well combined. Spoon the butter down the middle of a piece of plastic wrap, fold up the edges over the butter and roll the mixture into a log shape. Refrigerate until firm. Slice the butter into rounds and serve on top of 1 kg (2 lb 4 oz) barbecued lamb or beef.

Sun-dried tomato and basil butter

SERVES 6

Beat 125 g (4½ oz/½ cup) butter until light and creamy, then add 30 g (1 oz) finely chopped sun-dried tomatoes, 1 tablespoon finely shredded basil and 20 g (¾ oz) finely grated parmesan cheese and mix together well. Spoon the butter into small pots and swirl the surface with a flat-bladed knife. Serve on top of 1 kg (2 lb 4 oz) barbecued meats.

Sausage marinades

Apricot and onion marinade

MAKES ENOUGH FOR 1 KG (2 LB 4 OZ) SAUSAGES

Mix the following ingredients thoroughly in a bowl: 80 ml (2½ fl oz/⅓ cup) apricot nectar, 3 tablespoons lime marmalade, 2 crushed garlic cloves, 2 tablespoons olive oil, 1–2 tablespoons French onion soup mix, 1 tablespoon snipped chives, a dash of worcestershire sauce. Prick the sausages all over and marinate, covered, for at least 3 hours or overnight in the refrigerator before cooking on the barbecue. This mixture is also suitable for use as a baste.

Herb marinade

MAKES ENOUGH FOR 1 KG (2 LB 4 OZ) SAUSAGES

Mix the following ingredients thoroughly in a bowl: 60 ml (2 fl oz/¼ cup) olive oil, 2–3 tablespoons lemon juice or balsamic vinegar, 1–2 crushed garlic cloves, 3 teaspoons soft brown sugar, some salt and freshly ground black pepper and 4 tablespoons of chopped mixed herbs (use any combination you have handy—chives, lemon thyme, rosemary, parsley, basil, coriander (cilantro), mint, oregano or marjoram). Prick the sausages all over and marinate, covered, in a non-metallic dish for at least 3 hours or overnight in the refrigerator before cooking on the barbecue. Use with any type of sausage. This mixture is also suitable for use as a baste.

Honey and chilli marinade

MAKES ENOUGH FOR 1 KG (2 LB 4 OZ) SAUSAGES

Mix the following ingredients thoroughly in a bowl: 60 ml (2 fl oz/¼ cup) soy sauce, 1 tablespoon grated fresh ginger, 2 teaspoons grated lemon zest, 90 g (3¼ oz/¼ cup) honey, 1–2 crushed garlic cloves, 1 tablespoon sherry or rice wine and 3 tablespoons sweet chilli sauce. Prick the sausages all over and marinate, covered, in a non-metallic dish for at least 3 hours or overnight in the refrigerator before cooking on the barbecue. This marinade goes well with any kind of sausage. It is also suitable for basting.

Plum and coriander marinade

MAKES ENOUGH FOR 1 KG (2 LB 4 OZ) SAUSAGES

Mix the following ingredients thoroughly in a bowl: 60 ml (2 fl oz/¼ cup) plum sauce, 1–2 crushed garlic cloves, 1 tablespoon each of worcestershire and soy sauce, 2 tablespoons each of lime juice and chopped coriander (cilantro) and 60 ml (2 fl oz/¼ cup) tomato sauce (ketchup). Prick the sausages all over and marinate, covered, for at least 3 hours or overnight in the refrigerator before cooking on the barbecue. This mixture is also suitable for basting.

Spicy tandoori marinade

MAKES ENOUGH FOR 1 KG (2 LB 4 OZ) SAUSAGES

Mix the following ingredients thoroughly in a bowl: 1 tablespoon oil, 2 teaspoons each of ground cumin, coriander and paprika, 3 teaspoons turmeric, 2 teaspoons each of fresh grated ginger and tamarind sauce, 2 crushed garlic cloves, ½–1 teaspoon chilli powder, ½ teaspoon salt, 3 tablespoons tomato sauce (ketchup) and 200 g (7 oz) plain yoghurt. Prick the sausages all over and marinate, covered, for at least 3 hours or overnight in the refrigerator before cooking on the barbecue. Use for lamb or chicken sausages. This mixture is also suitable for basting.

Marinades and glazes for chicken

Honey soy marinade

MAKES ENOUGH FOR 1 KG (2 LB 4 OZ) CHICKEN PIECES

Mix 175 g (6 oz/½ cup) honey, 125 ml (4 fl oz/½ cup) soy sauce, 2 crushed garlic cloves, 4 tablespoons sake and 1 teaspoon Chinese five-spice powder in a bowl. Pour over 1 kg (2 lb 4 oz) chicken pieces and toss well. Cover and refrigerate for 2 hours or overnight before cooking on the barbecue.

Mexican marinade

MAKES ENOUGH FOR 1 KG (2 LB 4 OZ) CHICKEN PIECES

Combine 440 g (15½ oz) bottled taco sauce, 2 tablespoons lime juice and 2 tablespoons chopped coriander (cilantro) leaves. Pour the marinade over 1 kg (2 lb 4 oz) scored chicken pieces and toss well to combine. Cover and refrigerate for 2 hours or overnight before cooking on the barbecue.

Tandoori marinade

MAKES ENOUGH FOR 1 KG (2 LB 4 OZ) CHICKEN PIECES

Combine 4 tablespoons tandoori paste, 500 g (1 lb 2 oz) plain yoghurt and 2 tablespoons lime juice. Cut 1 kg (2 lb 4 oz) chicken pieces in half lengthways and thread onto skewers. Pour over the marinade and toss well to combine. Cover and refrigerate for 1–2 hours before cooking on the barbecue.

Thai marinade

MAKES ENOUGH FOR 1 KG (2 LB 4 OZ) CHICKEN PIECES

Combine 2 tablespoons fish sauce, 2 tablespoons lime juice, 1 crushed garlic clove, 1 finely chopped lemongrass stem (white part only), 2 teaspoons soft brown sugar, 125 ml (4 fl oz/½ cup) coconut cream and 2 tablespoons chopped coriander (cilantro) leaves. Pour the marinade over 1 kg (2 lb 4 oz) chicken pieces and toss well to combine. Cover and refrigerate for 2 hours or overnight before cooking on the barbecue.

Lime and ginger glaze

MAKES ENOUGH FOR 1 KG (2 LB 4 OZ) CHICKEN PIECES

Put 160 g (5¾ oz/½ cup) lime marmalade, 60 ml (2 fl oz/¼ cup) lime juice, 2 tablespoons sherry, 2 tablespoons soft brown sugar and 2 teaspoons finely grated fresh ginger in a saucepan. Stir over low heat until liquid. Pour over 1 kg (2 lb 4 oz) chicken pieces and toss well to combine. Cover and refrigerate for 2 hours or overnight before cooking on the barbecue.

Redcurrant glaze

MAKES ENOUGH FOR 1 KG (2 LB 4 OZ) CHICKEN PIECES

Put 680 g (1 lb 8 oz) redcurrant jelly, 4 tablespoons lemon juice, 4 tablespoons brandy and 2 teaspoons chopped thyme in a saucepan and stir over low heat until the mixture becomes liquid. Pour over 1 kg (2 lb 4 oz) chicken pieces and toss well to combine. Cover and refrigerate for 2 hours or overnight before cooking on the barbecue.

Butters, marinades and sauces for seafood

Lemon and dill butter

SERVES 6

Beat 90 g (3¼ oz/⅓ cup) butter with electric beaters until smooth. Beat in 2 teaspoons finely chopped dill, ½ teaspoon finely grated lemon zest and 2 tablespoons lemon juice until well combined. Spoon onto baking paper, shape into a log, roll up and twist the ends to seal. Refrigerate until firm, then cut into thick slices.

Olive, anchovy and caper butter

SERVES 6

Beat 125 g (4½ oz/½ cup) butter with electric beaters until smooth. Beat in 2 teaspoons chopped capers, 3–4 chopped anchovy fillets and 1 tablespoon finely chopped green olives. Spoon onto baking paper, shape into a log, roll up and twist the ends to seal. Refrigerate until firm, then cut into thick slices.

Pesto butter

SERVES 6

Place 4 tablespoons basil leaves, 1 tablespoon each of pine nuts and grated parmesan and 1 crushed garlic clove in a food processor or blender and process until smooth. Transfer to a bowl, add 125 g (4½ oz) butter and beat with a wooden spoon until combined. Spoon onto baking paper, shape into a log, roll up and twist the ends to seal. Refrigerate until firm, then cut into thick slices.

Roasted capsicum and rocket butter

SERVES 6

Beat 125 g (4½ oz/½ cup) butter with electric beaters until smooth. Fold through 1 large crushed garlic clove, 2 tablespoons finely chopped rocket (arugula) leaves, 1½ tablespoons finely chopped basil and ½ red capsicum (pepper), roasted, peeled and chopped. Spoon onto baking paper, shape into a log, roll up and twist the ends to seal. Refrigerate until firm, then cut into thick slices.

Saffron and parsley butter

SERVES 6

Grind ¼ teaspoon saffron threads in a mortar and pestle or spice grinder until powdery. Transfer to a small bowl, add 1 tablespoon hot water and soak for 2 minutes. Beat 125 g (4½ oz/½ cup) butter with electric beaters until smooth. Beat in 2 teaspoons finely chopped parsley and the saffron and water. Spoon onto baking paper, shape into a log, roll up and twist the ends to seal. Refrigerate until firm, then cut into thick slices.

Semi-dried tomato and white castello butter

SERVES 6

Beat 90 g (3¼ oz/⅓ cup) butter with electric beaters until smooth. Fold in 60 g (2¼ oz) finely chopped semi-dried tomatoes and 60 g (2¼ oz) chopped white castello cheese. Spoon onto baking paper, shape into a log, roll up and twist the ends to seal. Refrigerate until firm, then cut into thick slices.

Sweet chilli and coriander butter

SERVES 6

Beat 125 g (4½ oz/½ cup) butter with electric beaters until smooth. Beat in 2 tablespoons sweet chilli sauce, 1 tablespoon chopped coriander (cilantro), ½ teaspoon grated fresh ginger and 1–2 teaspoons fish sauce. Spoon onto baking paper, shape into a log, roll up and twist the ends to seal. Refrigerate until firm, then cut into thick slices.

Wasabi and seaweed butter

SERVES 6

Beat 125 g (4½ oz) butter with electric beaters until smooth. Fold through 2 teaspoons wasabi paste, 1 teaspoon rice vinegar and 1 sheet finely sliced nori (dried seaweed). Spoon onto baking paper, shape into a log, roll up and twist the ends to seal. Refrigerate until firm, then cut into thick slices.

Garlic marinade

MAKES ENOUGH FOR 1 KG (2 LB 4 OZ) | FOR PRAWNS (SHRIMP) AND FISH

Crush 6 garlic cloves and mix with 250 ml (9 fl oz/1 cup) extra virgin olive oil, 1 tablespoon lemon juice and 1 tablespoon chopped dill in a shallow, non-metallic dish. Add 1 kg (2 lb 4 oz) cubed firm white fish or peeled, deveined prawns (shrimp). Cover and refrigerate overnight. Return to room temperature, thread onto skewers and cook on a hot barbecue grill plate or flat plate until cooked through.

Lime and peppercorn marinade

MAKES ENOUGH FOR 1 KG (2 LB 4 OZ) | FOR PRAWNS (SHRIMP), FISH STEAKS AND CUTLETS SUCH AS TUNA, SWORDFISH, BLUE EYE, SALMON

Stir-fry 60 g (2¼ oz) sichuan or black peppercorns in a wok until fragrant. Transfer to a mortar and pestle or spice grinder, add 4 chopped red Asian shallots (eschalots) and crush together. Transfer to a shallow non-metallic dish and add 80 ml (2½ fl oz/⅓ cup) lime juice, 1 tablespoon salt, 1 teaspoon sesame oil and 60 ml (2 fl oz/¼ cup) peanut oil. Add 1 kg (2 lb 4 oz) firm white fish fillets or peeled, deveined prawns with tails intact. Cover; chill for 3 hours. Cook on a hot, lightly oiled barbecue grill plate or flat plate in batches until the seafood is cooked through. If you are using tuna or salmon, don't overcook it or it will be dry.

Spiced yoghurt marinade

MAKES ENOUGH FOR 1 KG (2 BL 4 OZ) | FOR FIRM-FLESHED FISH SUCH AS SNAPPER, BREAM, OCEAN PERCH, FLAKE

Combine 400 g (14 oz) yoghurt, 1 tablespoon each of grated fresh ginger, ground cumin, ground cinnamon, ground coriander and ground mace, 1–2 tablespoons each of grated lime zest and juice and 2 tablespoons chopped mint in a shallow non-metallic bowl. Add 1 kg (2 lb 4 oz) fish fillets, cover and refrigerate for 3 hours. Cook on a hot barbecue grill plate or flat plate until tender.

Sweet and spicy basting sauce

MAKES ENOUGH FOR 1 KG (2 LB 4 OZ) | FOR YABBIES, BUGS (FLAT-HEAD LOBSTERS) AND SCAMPI

Combine 250 ml (9 fl oz/1 cup) sweet chilli sauce, 2 crushed garlic cloves, 1–2 tablespoons lemon juice, 1 tablespoon peanut oil, 50 g (1¾ oz) melted butter and 2 tablespoons chopped coriander (cilantro) in a large bowl. Toss 1 kg (2 lb 4 oz) seafood in 1 tablespoon oil and cook in batches on a hot barbecue grill plate or flat plate, turning and basting frequently with the sauce. Serve with any left-over sauce.

Texan barbecue basting sauce

MAKES ENOUGH FOR 1 KG (2 LB 4 OZ) | FOR ALL SHELLFISH

Combine 250 ml (9 fl oz/1 cup) tomato sauce (ketchup), 6 dashes of Tabasco sauce, 3 chopped rehydrated chipotle chillies and 1 tablespoon each of vinegar and oil in a bowl. Use to baste while cooking 1 kg (2 lb 4 oz) prawns (shrimp), bugs (flat-head lobsters) or yabbies.

Thai marinade

MAKES ENOUGH FOR 1 KG (2 LB 4 OZ) | FOR OCTOPUS

Combine 125 ml (4 fl oz/½ cup) fish sauce, 4 finely shredded makrut (kaffir lime) leaves, 2–3 tablespoons grated palm sugar (jaggery) or brown sugar, the juice and zest of 2 limes and 1 teaspoon sesame oil in a non-metallic bowl. Add 1 kg (2 lb 4 oz) cleaned octopus and marinate overnight. Drain well. Cook over very high heat on a barbecue grill plate or flat plate, turning frequently, for 3 minutes or until cooked.

Butter sauce

MAKES ENOUGH FOR 1 KG (2 LB 4 OZ) | FOR BARBECUED LOBSTER TAIL

Finely chop two French shallots (eschalots) and place in a small saucepan with 60 ml (2 fl oz/¼ cup) each of white wine vinegar and water. Bring to the boil, then reduce the heat and simmer until reduced to 2 tablespoons. Remove from the heat and strain into a clean saucepan. Return to the heat and whisk in 220 g (7¾ oz) cubed unsalted butter, a few pieces at a time. The sauce will thicken as the butter is added. Season to taste with salt, pepper and lemon juice.

Cannellini bean and semi-dried tomato salsa

MAKES ENOUGH FOR 1 KG (2 LB 4 OZ) | FOR FISH SUCH AS RED MULLET OR SNAPPER

Drain a 400 g (14 oz) tin cannellini beans and rinse the beans. Put in a bowl and stir with 75 g (2½ oz/½ cup) chopped semi-dried tomatoes, 30 g (1 oz/¼ cup) sliced pitted black olives and ¼ red onion, chopped. Stir in 1 tablespoon olive oil, 3 teaspoons white wine vinegar and 1 tablespoon finely chopped flat-leaf (Italian) parsley. Cover and refrigerate for 30 minutes, or until required.

Creamy tarragon sauce

MAKES ENOUGH FOR 1 KG (2 LB 4 OZ) | FOR FIRM WHITE FISH, SUCH AS BLUE EYE

Combine 125 ml (4 fl oz/½ cup) fish stock in a small saucepan with 1 crushed garlic clove, 1 teaspoon dried tarragon leaves and 1 thinly sliced spring onion (scallion). Bring to the boil, then reduce the heat and simmer for 3 minutes, or until reduced by half. Add 250 ml (9 fl oz/1 cup) thick (double/heavy) cream or mascarpone cheese. Reduce the heat to very low and stir until the cream has fully melted. Add ½ teaspoon lemon juice, 2 tablespoons grated parmesan cheese and salt and black pepper to taste. Simmer for 1 minute, then serve.

Mango-avocado salsa

MAKES ENOUGH FOR 1 KG (2 LB 4 OZ) | FOR BARBECUED PRAWNS (SHRIMP)

Cut 1 mango and 1 avocado into small cubes and place in a small non-metallic bowl with 1 diced small red capsicum (pepper). Mix 2 tablespoons lime juice with 1 teaspoon caster (superfine) sugar and pour over the mango. Stir in 3 tablespoons chopped coriander (cilantro) leaves.

Roasted capsicum and basil sauce

MAKES ENOUGH FOR 1 KG (2 LB 4 OZ) | FOR BARBECUED SARDINES, SWORDFISH OR TUNA

Preheat the oven to 210°C (415°F/Gas 6–7). Halve two red capsicums (peppers) and place skin side up on a greased baking tray with two unpeeled garlic cloves. Brush with olive oil and bake for 20 minutes, or until the capsicum is soft and the skin has blackened and blistered. Remove and cool the capsicums in a plastic bag. Peel the capsicums and garlic and mix in a food processor or blender for 30 seconds, or until combined. With the motor running, slowly add 100 ml (3½ fl oz) olive oil in a thin stream and blend until all the oil is added and the mixture is smooth. Add 1 tablespoon finely chopped basil, ¼ teaspoon salt and black pepper. Serve warm or cold.

Salad dressings

Aïoli (garlic mayonnaise)

MAKES ABOUT 250 ML (9 FL OZ/1 CUP)

Mix together 250 ml (9 fl oz/1 cup) mayonnaise with 3 crushed garlic cloves. Season, to taste, with salt and pepper. Serve with barbecued seafood, such as prawns (shrimp).

Blue cheese dressing

MAKES ABOUT 250 ML (9 FL OZ/1 CUP)

Mix together 125 ml (4 fl oz/½ cup) mayonnaise, 60 ml (2 fl oz/¼ cup) thick (double/heavy) cream, 1 teaspoon white wine vinegar and 1 tablespoon finely snipped chives. Crumble 50 g (1¾ oz) blue cheese into the mixture and gently stir through. Season with salt and white pepper. Can be kept refrigerated, covered, for up to 2 days. Serve as a salad dressing or with barbecued asparagus.

Caesar dressing

MAKES ABOUT 185 ML (6 FL OZ/¾ CUP)

Cook an egg in boiling water for 1 minute. Break the egg into a small bowl and add 2 tablespoons white wine or tarragon vinegar, 2 teaspoons dijon mustard, 2 chopped anchovy fillets and 1 crushed garlic clove. Mix together with a small wire whisk. Add 125 ml (4 fl oz/½ cup) oil in a thin stream, whisking continuously until the mixture is smooth and creamy. Keep, covered, in the fridge for up to 2 days. Serve over crisp salad.

Cocktail sauce

MAKES ABOUT 310 ML (10¼ FL OZ/1¼ CUPS)

Mix together 250 ml (9 fl oz/1 cup) mayonnaise, 3 tablespoons tomato sauce (ketchup), 2 teaspoons worcestershire sauce, ½ teaspoon lemon juice and 1 drop of Tabasco sauce. Season with salt and pepper. Keep, covered, in the fridge for up to 2 days.

Green goddess dressing

MAKES ABOUT 412 ML (14½ FL OZ/1⅔ CUPS)

Mix together 375 ml (13 fl oz/1½ cups) mayonnaise, 4 mashed anchovy fillets, 4 finely chopped spring onions (scallions), 1 crushed garlic clove, 1 medium handful chopped flat-leaf (Italian) parsley, 3 tablespoons finely snipped chives and 1 teaspoon tarragon vinegar. Serve on salad or with barbecued seafood.

Mayonnaise

MAKES ABOUT 250 ML (9 FL OZ/1 CUP)

Whisk together 2 egg yolks, 1 teaspoon dijon mustard and 1 tablespoon lemon juice for 30 seconds, or until light and creamy. Add 185 ml (6 fl oz/¾ cup) olive oil, about a teaspoon at a time, whisking continuously. You can add the oil more quickly as the mayonnaise thickens. Season to taste with salt and white pepper. Alternatively, place the egg yolks, mustard and lemon juice in a food processor and mix for 10 seconds. With the motor running, add the oil in a thin stream. Season to taste.

Tartare sauce

MAKES ABOUT 412 ML (14½ FL OZ/1⅔ CUPS)

Mix together 375 ml (13 fl oz/1½ cups) mayonnaise, 1 tablespoon finely chopped onion, 1 teaspoon lemon juice, 1 tablespoon chopped gherkins (pickles), 1 teaspoon chopped capers, ¼ teaspoon dijon mustard and 1 tablespoon finely chopped parsley. Mix and season with salt and pepper. Top with a few capers and serve with barbecued seafood.

Thousand island dressing

MAKES 412 ML (14½ FL OZ/1⅔ CUPS)

Mix together 375 ml (13 fl oz/1½ cups) mayonnaise, 1 tablespoon sweet chilli sauce, 1–2 tablespoons tomato sauce (ketchup), ¼ red capsicum (pepper) and ¼ green capsicum (pepper), finely chopped, 1 tablespoon snipped chives and ½ teaspoon sweet paprika. Stir well and season. Cover and refrigerate for up to 3 days. Thousand Island dressing is traditionally served on lettuce leaves.

Cooking techniques

Indirect cooking

Indirect cooking on a covered kettle barbecue brand roasts or bakes food more slowly than direct cooking. Fragrant wood chips can be added to the coals to give the food more flavour (see images below).

To prepare for indirect cooking:
1. Remove the lid. Open bottom vent.
2. Put the bottom grill inside the bowl and attach charcoal rails. Heap coals in rails. Put firelighters inside coals.
3. Light fire, leaving lid off. When coals reach fine-ash stage, put a drip-tray or baking dish on bottom grill. Position top grill; add food.

To prepare for smoking:
1. Prepare the barbecue as above.
2. When the coals reach fine-ash stage, add wood chips, fill a drip tray with 1 litre (35 fl oz/4 cups) hot water and cover with a lid until fragrant smoke develops.
3. Centre food on top grill and cover.

Direct cooking

As with grilling or frying in the kitchen, the less turning or handling of the food the better. Once the fire is ready, lightly brush the barbecue grill plate or flat plate with oil. Place the food over the hottest part of the fire and sear quickly on both sides—this will help the food retain its moisture by sealing the surface. Once seared, move the food to a cooler part of the hotplate to cook for a few more minutes. Barbecuing is a fast-cooking process so even well-done food will not take very long. The barbecue flat plate is also ideal for stir-frying.

Test meat for 'doneness' by firmly pressing it with tongs or the flat edge of a knife. Meat that is ready to serve should 'give' slightly but not resist pressure too easily. At first, you may find it difficult to judge, but try to resist cutting or stabbing the meat—this not only reduces its succulence by releasing the juices, but the juices can also cause the fire to flare.

While beef and lamb can be cooked from rare to well-done, according to your personal taste, pork and chicken should never be served rare. If you are in any doubt whether they are cooked through, remove to a separate plate and make a slight cut in the thickest part of the meat. If the juices do not run clear, return to the heat for further cooking.

Test fish for doneness by gently flaking back the flesh in the thickest part with a fork. Cooked flesh should be white and opaque, but still moist.

Safety

Barbecues involve open flames, crowds of people and, often, alcohol, so it is a good idea to keep a few safety tips in mind.

Keep a hose or bucket of water close by. A fire extinguisher or fire blanket is more suitable if you intend to use your barbecue regularly. Never light a barbecue with a flammable liquid, instead always use firelighters or light up some twigs and paper.

Light the fire and leave the lid off to allow the coals to reach fine-ash stage.

Place a drip tray underneath the top grill when the coals are ready.

For smoking, spoon a generous quantity of smoking chips over the hot coals.

Index

Index

Published in 2008 by Murdoch Books Pty Limited.

Murdoch Books Australia
Pier 8/9, 23 Hickson Road
Millers Point NSW 2000
Phone: + 61 (0) 2 8220 2000
Fax: + 61 (0) 2 8220 2558
www.murdochbooks.com.au

Murdoch Books UK Limited
Erico House, 6th Floor
93–99 Upper Richmond Road
Putney, London SW15 2TG
Phone: + 44 (0) 20 8785 5995
Fax: + 44 (0) 20 8785 5985
www.murdochbooks.co.uk

Chief Executive: Juliet Rogers
Publishing Director: Kay Scarlett

Project manager and editor: Paul O'Beirne
Design concept: Heather Menzies
Design: Heather Menzies and Jacqueline Richards
Photographer: Alan Benson
Stylist: Mary Harris
Food preparation: Christopher Tate
Introduction text: Leanne Kitchen
Production: Nikla Martin

National Library of Australia Cataloguing-in-Publication Data
Home Style Barbecue. Includes index.
ISBN 978 1 74196 170 6 (pbk.).
1. Barbecue cookery. I. Title. 641.76

A catalogue record for this book is available from the British Library.

Colour separation by Splitting Image in Clayton, Victoria, Australia.
Printed by i-Book Printing Ltd. in 2008. PRINTED IN CHINA.

IMPORTANT: Those who might be at risk from the effects of salmonella poisoning
(the elderly, pregnant women, young children and those suffering from immune deficiency diseases)
should consult their doctor with any concerns about eating raw eggs.

CONVERSION GUIDE: You may find cooking times vary depending on the oven
you are using. For fan-forced ovens, as a general rule, set the oven temperature to
20°C (35°F) lower than indicated in the recipe.